Apprehended:
The Trials of Dickie Lynn

By Domingo Soto

Copyright 2013 Domingo Soto

ISBN: 978-1-304-20189-8

Published by

Easter Publishing
465 Dauphin Street
Mobile, Alabama 36602

Other Easter Publications:

Mobile: American River City
by Michael Thomason and Melton McLaurin,
1975

ON MOBILE STREETS: a rumor of the city
by Jackson Hill,
1978

To our children. You pay for our mistakes.

4321

CONTENTS

1	The Jungle	1
2	The Keys	3
3	The Border	6
4	Salad Days	10
5	Getting It Together	13
6	Heart of Dixie	18
7	Freedom Fighters	22
8	The Hartley Boys	28
9	Vaiden Field	35
10	Stephen Bishop	40
11	Local Boy	44
12	Ground Control	46
13	Cowboy Bob	49
14	Show Time	52
15	Ground Crew	60
16	The Big Cheese-Eater	65
17	The Consigliere	76
18	Kevin	83
19	Another Insider	89
20	The Scent Gets Stronger	94
21	Backup	100
22	Abbott	104
23	Trial, An Error	107
24	A Taste of Honey	118
25	Double Down	122
26	Andy	124
27	Charlie Jordan	128
28	Ricou Redux	133
29	Holding the Bag	137
30	Mercy?	148
	Postscript	159
	Chronology	165

Preface

Instant buzz kill. It's my secretary. "Richard Lynn," she says. Before I can make an excuse not to answer it, she is gone. I man up, compose myself and answer the call. I expect the same angry voice that I had encountered ten years before when, after managing a call to the Florence Supermax Prison where he was doing life, he had rejected my request. I wanted, I had told him then, to write a story about his case. "Leave me out of it," he told me curtly. So, I dropped it. Dickie Lynn, even if locked up and doing time in one of this country's most draconian institutions wasn't anyone I wanted to roil, even if I thought it a great story. I had better things to do with my time.

Before I became a lawyer, I was a different kind of tale spinner. I had been a rebel, a radical and a rabble rouser in college, editor of our college newspaper, underground journalist, a reporter for the local daily and then I did another seven years as the founder and publisher of a weekly. Luckily, those were good credentials for the legal services office that was opening in Mobile. I sold my newspaper and worked four and a half years as a public benefits paralegal. I followed that with my three years at the University of Alabama School of Law. It was now 1986. I was forty years old and beginning a second career. Again, though, I got lucky. It had never been my intention to practice criminal law. I had envisioned being a different sort of champion, doing civil rights, discrimination or labor law. But I managed to partner with my legal services mentor and friend. Since he did criminal law, I did too. His remarkable ability and esteemed reputation, coupled with my ability to speak Spanish, moved our firm to the head of the line and I soon found myself involved in some of the most high-profile cases in our area.

One of those was the Dickie Lynn case. Not more than three years out of law school, I was trying a case that involved sixteen tons of cocaine, some of the best lawyers in the country, and "sexy" facts. The case involved a well-oiled machine of high-end and affluent pretty-boy Florida Keys drug traffickers who routinely traveled here to a command center they had set up in a rural hunting camp. With the precision of a military unit, they would use sophisticated radio communications equipment to triangulate communications between Florida and South and Central America and orchestrate the many moving parts of their scheme. The aircraft would depart from Miami and arrive in Columbia at the same time as the contraband. There would be someone in Belize to refuel the plane. In Alabama, an impromptu landing field would be constructed moments before the plane's arrival. Offloaders would arrive from other parts of the country. Within minutes the contraband and the field were gone. This synchronicity had resulted in the importation of huge amounts of cocaine "up the 88," the line of longitude that runs through Mobile.

The Lynn case had an enormous impact on me. I represented an offloaded who refused to plead even though it meant facing a trial alongside "Drug Kingpins." And not just that. There were allegations of horrendous facts that included dead pilots, supposed death threats, claymore mines, guns, and nasty Third World characters. Truth be told, my client's insistence on going to trial tickled me. I was a new lawyer and now had a major case to try. Because he was such a minor figure my task was easy, stay the hell out of the way and let the big dogs fight.

The trial lasted five weeks. It was a wonderful training opportunity for me. Better yet, my client was acquitted. While we waited for the jury to deliberate, I tried another short trial and won it. I took my "not guilty" verdict in front of some superstar Miami lawyers. I came out as energized as the battery bunny. I had gotten two federal trial acquittals in two days and was now officially hooked on drugs and crime. I tried two other high-profile cases shortly after that and the skills that I had learned in the Lynn case helped establish me. I had my niche.

But that wasn't the end of the Lynn case. It never seemed to want to go away. We had spent five weeks in the courtroom: judge, prosecutor, agents, defense lawyers, and, of course, the defendants. I think we all felt a little kinship with each other after having been involved in this big of a case. I certainly did. These defendants were mostly kids caught in a horrible vice and the sentences they received were off-the-charts. They would waltz in and out of the court system in Mobile for many more years, trying to cut their losses, asking for mercy but only sometimes getting it. Mobile being the proverbial small pond, I would notice.

The appellate decision was also remarkable. The Eleventh Circuit Court of Appeals is highly government-friendly and, yet, ruled in the defendants' favor. I had witnessed firsthand the prosecutor's supposed infraction and thought that maybe the appellate court was trying to ameliorate a bad result at her expense. I'm not given to pitying prosecutors but I thought that she had gotten a bum rap. Lynn, too, I thought had gotten the short end of the stick, even if it was a self-inflicted wound. It maintained my interest in the case. I kept up with Lynn's efforts to get re-sentenced. I called him and he told me to go to hell so it all died down. We all just went on our merry ways. Dickie was out of my mind.

Then, a few years ago I got a call from my offloaded client's daughter. She wanted to know more about her dad. He had passed away and she was looking for some closure. She wanted information about the trial. I had spent probably the most important part of his life with him and we had become confidants and friends. She and I chatted for awhile. I told her that I had the trial transcript and promised her I would look at it and get back in touch with her. When I finally got around to rereading the transcript, I was back in the moment. I decided to write something. I wrote a movie script but the finished product felt incomplete. Like a script, it was only the interstices of a really complex story. I researched the players. I ordered the file from the national archive. Sure enough, the story had some enormous depth to it.

The agents had been the real heroes of this drama. They had tenaciously developed a case from a lot of loose ends and disparate places and it had resulted in many successful prosecutions. I hoped that enough time had passed that one of them would be willing to talk to me. My first thought was Ed Odom. He had been the major player in this prosecution. We had worked some major cases together over the years, he was always professional, gracious and, most importantly, genuine. I gave it a shot. After all, all he could say was "no." Amazingly, he agreed to do an interview with me. What I discovered was that he and I were on the same page. He didn't like the way the case ultimately played out.

But, unlike the others, Odom had never abandoned the search for a righteous ending. He had stayed in touch with Dickie, hoping to right what he perceived as an injustice. It was Ed who "dropped the dime" on me by snitching to Dickie that I was writing a story about the case. That's how Dickie came to be calling me on the phone. "Hello, Dominick," he said. I held my breath for what I knew was sure to be a tongue-lashing and a warning to leave things alone. But it was a different guy on the phone. He had made peace with his devils. Time had mellowed him. He was cheery and wanted to know how he could assist me. Some of it is serendipity and some of it is naked calculation, but the person on the other end of the phone was not the same person I had spoken to a decade ago. We started talking. I went to visit him and he helped fill me in on the questions I had about the group's inner workings.

If we are truly capable of change, we can deserve forgiveness. Dickie has been in prison for more than two decades. Some might agree with the life sentence meted out to him, especially at first blush. What I think I show here is that good cause exists for thinking that Dickie's case deserves to be revisited. Concerned that the justice system was "being played," there has been for the last twenty years a national trend to make it intractable, to limit options, to bank on the concrete, to diminish the human calculus and the balancing of the merits of things. The subjective is now officially discounted. The measures of humaneness and humanity are seen as too ethereal.

This notion of "certainty" is a conceit that more often than not serves to thwart a just result. The justice system is a machine whose fodder is people. And its moving parts are people. They can be just as subjective in the application of the system. They, too, are prey to human foible, something that I think is prevalent in this case. Justice has not only turned its blind eye to what Dickie has done to ameliorate the wrongs he has committed, it is being wrongfully vengeful and petty. This is not a legal tome. Yes, it's a lawyer's war story and an account of a drug prosecution, a true crime tale. But, more than that, it's an allegory about justice, injustices and the justice system.

June 13-89 16:24   DEA MOB RO

Case number: GQ - 88 - 2002 (OCDETF)

U.S. Department of Justice
Drug Enforcement Administration

REPORT OF INVESTIGATION

1. Program Code	2. Cross File	Related Files	3. File No.	4. G-DEP Identifier
5. By:			6. File Title	
7. ☐ Closed ☐ Requested Action Completed ☐ Action Requested By:			8. Date Prepared	
9. Other Officers:				
10. Report				

DEFENDANT ROLE IN ORGANIZATION/DUTIES AND THREAT OF EACH TO OTHERS:

1.) **Richard Joseph LYNN** - Head of organization that has imported approximately 16,000 kilograms of cocaine into the United States from South America since early 1980's. Has amassed large cash reserves which are mostly hidden in off-shore or European banks. Has access to and has utilized false identification since his early involvement. Has criminal contacts in South America and Central America and Mexico as well as in the Florida Keys and the Hispanic community of South Florida.

   LYNN should be considered a great escape risk. LYNN has many friends and associates both inside the prison system and outside. It would not be out of character for LYNN to stage an elaborate escape attempt.

   LYNN has utilized firearms during the commission of drug felonies. At the time of Lynn's arrest two AK-47 assault rifles were seized from his residence. A very large amount of live ammunition was also seized. In the past, LYNN has indicated a willingness to murder law enforcement officers if they attempted to arrest him or his associates. LYNN is believed to have been involved in a bomb/murder in Sebring, Florida and attempted to employ a co-defendant to murder a cooperating witness for $150,000.00 (this occurred the day before LYNN's arrest).

2.) **Ricou Grey DESHAW** - At one time was Richard LYNN's equal in the above organization. Later formed his own smuggling group in South Florida. Fled the U.S. and went to Austria after a grand jury subpoena was issued for him. Has a commercial pilot's license and is qualified in commercial jets. Has numerous contacts in the National Football League and in South and Central American countries, Mexico, and the Bahamas.

   DESHAW should be considered an escape/flee risk: A cooperating witness/defendant had threats made against his family in Alabama shortly after DESHAW's arrest.

3.) **Butch William MCKEOWN** - Presently under indictment in the Southern District of Florida, with an additional indictment in the same district pending. Owner of a gun shop (has a federal firearms license) and communications equipment shop in the Florida Keys.

MCKEOWN worked for the organization as a communications electronics expert. He checked load aircraft for the presence of law enforcement tracking devices prior to a trip; maintained high frequency radio communications for the organization by maintaining contact with the load aircraft, the strip in Colombia, South America, the refueling site in Belize, Central America, and the offload strip in Alabama. Also provided radios and police scanners and frequency list. Provided cellular telephones in false names to key members of this organization.

At arraignment in Mobile, MCKEOWN made threatening gestures toward co-defendant believed to be cooperating with government.

4.) **Robert Irving EYSTER** - Minor role as communications operator. Worked for MCKEOWN in this organization. Usually went to the off-load site in Alabama with communications equipment. Maintained contact with aircraft and refuel and load strips. Also manned scanners monitoring law enforcement traffic.

Doesn't appear to be a great risk/threat.

5.) **Jack Leroy MARSHALL**- A biker that owns/operates the RATSASS CUSTOM BIKE SHOP in St. Cloud, Florida. Has numerous criminal contacts and associates in outlaw motorcycle gangs.

MARSHALL should be considered a great escape risk. Information has been received through an investigation by DEA, Miami, that MARSHALL had at his mother's residence in St. Cloud, at the time of his arrest, large numbers of weapons and ammunition and a large amount of C4 plastic explosive.

MARSHALL was employed by LYNN in the organization to be security at the offload sites.

MARSHALL was to kill any law enforcement officers that attempted to arrest those on the airstrip. MARSHALL also provided armed security during the transportation of the cocaine from Alabama to South Florida.

MARSHALL has used numerous alias names and had false identification on his person at the time of his arrest.

6.) **Steven Gorton PURVIS** - Employed by LYNN as one of his top operators. PURVIS handled keeping the crews together, offloading the cocaine, refueling the aircraft in Alabama, and transporting the cocaine.

PURVIS divorced his wife approximately six months ago, according to CI's, in order to move all assets from his name. Has made the statement "what's one more load, if

I'm looking at 30 years now." At the time of his arrest, PURVIS stated he lives out of his pickup truck.

PURVIS should be considered an escape risk and a threat to cooperating defendants' witnesses.

7.) **David C. DAVENPORT** - COOPERATING DEFENDANT/WITNESS - Has been threatened by LYNN and Marshall.

At the time of Davenport's arrest, he was armed with a silenced .22 pistol. He surrendered a case of C4 explosives and four Claymore anti-personnel mines to arresting officers. Has past military experience including Vietnam experience as U. S. Army Special Forces/Ranger.

Could be an escape risk. SHOULD BE SEGREGATED FROM OTHER DEFENDANTS (except Robert Wardle)

8.) **Robert Wardle, III** - Partner of David DAVENPORT - COOPERATING DEFENDANT - Also has extensive military experience- Special Forces/Ranger Officer (1st.Lt.), Vietnam veteran.

Along with DAVENPORT, provided security at refueling strips in Belize, Central America.

9.) **Jay Hilery DEWEESE** - Occupied same level in organization as did PURVIS. Has prior conviction/incarceration. Utilized firearms in security position at offload site in Alabama. Delivered threat on alleged witness in South Florida.

Due to age, any sentence tantamount to life sentence. Should be considered an escape risk and threat to any and all cooperating defendants/witnesses.

10.) **Christian W. SCHMIDGALL** - Operated as a transporter of the cocaine from Alabama to South Florida. Attempted cooperation with U. S. Coast Guard in order to maintain inside information of interdiction efforts of U.S. Gov't.

He is a pilot and has extensive contacts in South and Central America.

DEA SENSITIVE
Drug Enforcement Administration

This report is the property of the Drug Enforcement Administration.
Neither it nor its contents may be disseminated outside the agency to which loaned.

GLOSSARY

"After the Triumph of the Revolution"
Cubans, at least those on the island, describe events by epochs. This rather cumbersome term, meaning something post-1959, is used almost reverentially and is never shortened in conversations, no matter how casual or informal.

Alzados
To *alzar* is to raise, elevate, rise up or lift up.

Barbudo, el
The bearded one. Castro and his men took refuge in the mountains and didn't have the luxury of razors so they sported beards. That soon became a class symbol with Los Barbudos becoming both a derisive and affectionate way to describe them.

Brigadista
A member of a brigade, here, the literacy campaign.

Brigada 2506
One of the organizations fighting against the Cuban government.

Cada Otra Pendejada
Okay, this one takes some explaining. A *pendejo* is a pubic hair and is used to describe someone who is more than a *tonto* (a fool). A *pendejada* is something irksome and or miniscule. But, in this context, it is something quite vexing and carries a lot of emotional weight, like "every other fucking thing."

la Campaña Nacional de Alfabetización en Cuba
The National Literacy Campaign of Cuba.

Campesino
The *campo* is the country and *campesinos* live in the country, mostly as agricultural workers or rural poor. They are Latin America's Everymen.

Casa Particular
Private homes that are licensed to rent rooms to tourists.

Gusano
A worm, the epithet used by the Castroites to describe the Miami Cubans.

Jineterismo
A *jinete* is a jockey or ranger and *jineterismo* is the prevalent ad-hoc prostitution that sprang up in Cuba after the "Special Period."

Movimiento de Recuperación Democrática (MRD)
Movement for the Restoration of Democracy.

Nuyorican
A Puerto Rican raised in New York (actually, the East).

Plantados
To "plant" oneself, to become implacable, immovable.

Puto
Literally, a (male) prostitute, but, in this context, a little "bitch," a wimp.

The "Special Period"
The depression Cuba suffered with the collapse of the Soviet Union.

"Yo sí puedo"
Yes, I can!

Chapter 1
The Jungle

The men fidget below the forest canopy. They are *in defilade,* a fancy military term that means that their position is not exposed, that they are hidden and have melted into their surroundings. They strain to hear, endlessly it seems to them, beyond the silence and above the quiet, a quiet that they have so artificially imposed on the jungle. They wait. Their call to action will be the first faint drone of an approaching small aircraft. And with, at last, radio contact - "Two minutes out!" - they are "go." They carry torches down to the cane field road that they have transformed into a primitive runway and fire up the honor guard of large coffee cans. These "light pots" contain oil-soaked toilet paper rolls that nibble at the darkness and cast a flickering golden glow onto a macabre vignette. A fleet of laden vehicles and a bevy of armed men hug a wall of dancing sugarcane, the approaching plane its backdrop. Even before "Snoopy" has fully stopped, the operation enters metastasis. With a clockwork efficiency borne of practice and necessity no NASCAR pit crew could ever hope to match, the plane is taxied, stopped, spun around, tail numbers changed and they are again "go" and "Snoopy" is "out," and he is gone.

On the other side, men also wait. A communications post directs them from a third site. It keeps them posted on the positions of the pilots. Security is vigilant and ready. The load vehicles move into their positions. After days of interminable waiting, a pre-coital twenty-minute foreplay of fevered preparations, and a relapse into the forced dullness of anxious anticipation, sitting, waiting, and listening, now, finally, "Snoopy" buzzes nearby. He is home.

The plane is only a few minutes out. "Buckwheat" has been watching the dense fog roll in. He warns the pilot. "I can't even see the light from the paper mill. It might be a hard land." But Snoopy waves him off. After all, this isn't his first day at the rodeo. "I've got you. I can see the strip and everything." Buckwheat gives it another shot. "Hey, we've got the spotlight. We can turn it on." But, no, he is still unconcerned. "Forget it. I got it. Now, don't talk to me anymore." And that's what they do. They leave him alone. And wait. The swamp carries noise. They hear the plane for a very long time. A very long time. And at long last, they feel its presence as it flies overhead towards the field for what feels like yet another eternity.

A ball of fire expels the night. And like the flashlight prop at a campfire ghost story, the kinetic strobe captures the backlit Kodak moment of horror on their faces. Their vehicles race towards the crash site but there is nothing that can be done for these poor souls and they know that they must go, that there is little time, that they must leave their friends here. Their egress is blocked by the wreckage. The larger vehicle pushes out the side gate. They dissolve into the darkness. They run.

They run back to the place whose very name means color and brightness and flora and fauna, to a place that they know, where it is always a bit of paradise and a lot of everywhere, a place where everyone knows everyone else and the kids all grow up knowing everything about the outdoors and wholesome things, like sports, and boats, and fishing, and planes and, obviously, the water.

Chapter 2
The Keys

Richard "Dickie" Lynn grew up here in this little archipelago that begins at the tip of Florida, on the part called the Upper Keys. The youngest of three children, he is the product of the union of Esther Elizabeth Viedt and Walter Elihu Lynn. Esther, a big beautiful blonde of German descent had grown up on a farm in Middletown, Ohio. The Viedts raised this clan of nine girls and two boys to be self-sufficient. They planted it, hoed it, picked it, cooked and canned it. And, as a result, Esther became a great cook who could make the best of all the "peasant foods" associated with the area, things like toast pot roasts, stews, grits and oatmeal.

Raised in Michigan, Walter was a big 275 pound no-nonsense man who loved to hunt and fish. He had weathered the Depression by bagging deer that he and the local butcher would dress, clean, grind into hamburger and share with the locals. He was a boxer, so he wasn't one to shy away from a problem. He worked hard his entire life. He played just as hard. He didn't shy away from a drink, either, though it was mostly beer. He was neither a drunk nor a bully.

Walter's bronchitis pushed the Lynns southward, relocating to Tavernier Key when Dickie was only four years old. There wasn't much there in those days, just your usual mom and pop fish camps, small stores and eateries. One of those was the iconic Keys eatery, Manny and Isa's Kitchen. Manny Ortiz had been the cook at the Green Turtle when he finally decided to go on his own. He looked at a piece of property the Pinders had out on Matecumbe Key. It was perfect. In 1965 Manny and his wife opened at mile marker 81 on Islamorada. They had their own Key Lime grove and would soon become legend for their Key Lime pie, fried lobster, Cuban food and, of course, the ubiquitous Keys favorite, conch.

Patrons could count on getting great food, maybe seeing Ted Williams who was known to haunt this his favorite place and being waited on by Dickie's mom, Esther, who worked there for 18 years.

With his hazel eyes and brown hair and the chiseled good looks of a young Nick Nolte, Dickie looked like a regular all-American heartthrob. Although he had his mother's looks, he had his father's physique and most of his irascible traits. Dickie remembers his dad as a big brute of a man, a man with a huge appetite for life and an insatiable love of the outdoors. "He used to say that you're closer to God just being outside." Walter loved hunting and fishing and, because they were close, he was often accompanied by his young son, Dickie. Initially, they had a fish-smoking business and Dickie would tag along with his father. They would pick up fish when the boats docked and take them to the two giant smokers they had at their house. "I can remember as a 12-year-old going to school and everyone telling me that I smelled like smoke."

While most kids pester their parents to let them drive the family car, Dickie sought to take out his dad's 18-foot skiff. "He told me that when I was big enough to crank the 40-horsepower Gayle outboard I could take it out. I used to pull on the cord with all my might. I would pull and pull but I couldn't do it. One day my father is sitting out there drinking beer with his friends at Rusty's Fish Camp. I go by in the boat, waving to him as I go out the harbor. They all cheered and laughed." His father now tasked him with the job of disposing of the fish carcasses. This had a "baited field" effect on the fish. Soon the 13-year-old was renting out boats and taking the tourists out to his sweet fishing spots.

He knew his way around the waters and was a complete homeboy. He and his chums all went to Coral Shores School, the one school here. They spent their time doing what most kids here do. They fished, boated, or maybe for a little excitement they would lurk under one of the many bridges that link these little islands and jump on the back of a Manta Ray for a free ride. They played sports. His dad was the Little League coach and they even had Ted Williams, the major league ball player, as their mentor. The kids called him "Teddy Baseball." He endorsed sporting gear for Sears and Roebuck and, according to Dickie, would bring them all sorts of new fishing rods and reels and anything new that Sears wanted him to test, gloves and bats, and just give them to the local kids. "He came to our little league practices and games and showed us how to swing a bat, slide into a base, steal bases, throw the ball, *et cetera*. He was a great guy and loved his fishing."

Dickie's father eventually went into the construction industry and Lynn followed him into that too. But he was always around boats and had an unusual affinity for the water. When his father died in a Keys Highway car accident, Dickie quit school and soon thereafter married his high school sweetie, segueing this good life into adulthood.

Chapter 3
The Border

At nearby Boca Chica Naval Air Station, it is dawn and a young airman walks the flight line of an enclave carved out here for the Air Force at this country's southern frontier. He shivers and mutters to himself, wondering how it is that his dumb *nuyorican* ass is freezing even though he's wearing a B-3 flight jacket and the weather is no lower than the mid-60s. He is used to Northern winters. But, yeah, here he was, his wimpy self shivering like some little *puto*. But this Key West early morning chill is nothing. Really. It is transient and the sun will soon burn it away. Not so, his implacable boredom. The inner city doesn't give you much of an appreciation for fishing or the outdoors and that's about all there is to do here. Oh yeah, and drinking in the bars of a small town bursting at the seams with young men.

The Cold War is still a hot issue here and Cuba clearly is its focus. Nearby at Cudjoe Key, there is another Air Force unit with Spanish-surnamed personnel who refuse to acknowledge even a hello from a fellow service mate. Many of the civilians that work at Key West Naval Air are Cuban. All Cubans are freedom fighters, they'll tell you. The region was ground zero for the missile crisis and the Bay of Pigs invasion. The Cuban Brigade 2506 bombers had secretly set off from this and other nearby bases. And, that's the history behind the presence of Detachment 1. It is here to keep watch of our southern frontier, even if they do it in comfort. After all, this is the last vestige of the exalted Flying Tigers and the only unit in the Air Defense Command with an actual fighter mission. They are the stuff of war, a squadron of men who coddle six fighter jets, ever-vigilant and standing here at the tip of the Keys, just in case *El Barbudo* wants to start any crap, so close that they can actually watch Cuban television.

"Det 1" is a post eagerly sought after at their Florida Panhandle home base. Not only are they stationed in beautiful Key West, the digs are sumptuous by GI standards and they are isolated in every way from the Navy and its insistence on doing things in military ways. They are housed in a self-contained and fortified command center that looks and feels more like a hotel than a barracks. They sleep in two-man rooms with fancy furniture. They have their own kitchen and cook staff. No Navy chow. No squid discipline. They are about as pampered a unit as ever existed in the military. Even their on-duty hours are nothing more than patrolling an area not much larger than five city blocks or doing support work for only six jets and a small personnel unit. Mostly, it's interminable hours of Day Room ping pong and pool and the only real action that they ever see are the weekend intramural bar fights with the squids and the jar heads and the hunt for what is here a rarity, women.

Watching television in the day room at Boca, the airman watches a Castro speech on television and is blind-sided by the charisma of the man. He is stunned at the brilliance of his logic, the eloquence, the force and the magnitude of the man and finds himself in an emotional double bind because, after all, he is our enemy. And this particular enemy of his is a 600-man crack unit that constantly practices for war. They must be ready at a second's notice to engage in an IG inspection, replete with all sorts of scenarios and inventions designed to test their mettle. They will monitor each other's roentgens, estimating radiation load limits and life expectancies so that they can gauge who next to send out into the inferno and who is next to die.

Most of the time it turns out to be nothing, some numbnut wandering into the forbidden airspace, but they have no time for what-ifs. They must get the birds up and protect their pilots, the guys who daily do the really dangerous work. They have had the gruesome task of recovering one of their guys after his plane crashed at the end of the runway and it is a recurring topic. Another pilot out on one of these wild goose chases, completely disappeared into the water after telling his wing man that he was flying lower to inspect a bogie. This is the real deal.

But, mostly, it's ennui.

He visits a childhood friend, a running buddy from the same mean streets who is now a gung-ho Marine and stationed here at Boca Chica. He is stunned by the wounds that just about every man in the Marine barracks has. Bullets and shrapnel have left so many welts and tears and scars on their magnificent bodies. These really young men are now veterans of who knows what horrors. They proudly brandish these war mementos and fawn over their weapons and talk about experiences that to him only sound scary. And now that they're here in this little piece of heaven they eagerly volunteer to ride off-duty shotgun for Coast Guard coastal patrols, vying with each other to go on these trips, to outdo each other with stories about drug smuggler and Cuban gun runner skirmishes, automatic weapons fire fights and chases and all sorts of high testosterone *Miami Vice* stories. And they are true.

It has dawned into a beautiful Florida Keys day. The sun is shining. Dazzlingly brilliant, it has married the scale of the sky to the expanse of the seas. The candle flames of sailboats dance. Pleasure boats drone and dart about persistently. Like water bugs. Further out, large sea vessels plow. There appears to be no special import to the small flotilla of power boats that have set out that day. The boats race out, meandering towards a point where they will meet. They are a pirate crew meeting the mother ship. A freighter that is en route to Miami will rendezvous with them. It will be a brief encounter and they will scurry away, scuttling back to shore with their cargo.

They know to be vigilant because the coast is locked and loaded. There are two military installations in the area and the Coast Guard and the DEA's tethered blimp, "Fat Albert." But the boys in the drug boats are bathed in the seeming invulnerability of their youths. They wait for the mother ship knowing that they have the home-field advantages of proximity and cover and, most importantly, opportunity. They live near these "source of supply" countries. They hang with these foreigners in the nearby polyglot communities. And, they don't have far to go once they get their hands on the shipment. Their boats will mingle with the other boats and go back to their homes to unload their cargo. Not that this is some sort of *ad hoc* operation. They have a system and an experienced crew and in a residence at Lighthouse Point a radio room monitors the situation, communicates with the boats and does counter-surveillance.

The klaxons blare and Det 1 scrambles. The airmen don't know what's up, but, like an aroused ant bed, they scurry to their posts wondering if this is just one more stupid drill or something real. They will know soon enough by what they encounter. If it is a drill, there will be some stranger telling them that so and so has been blown up or that this or that is blocked, that they must cut a hole in the fence, or climb over the barbed wire and they can set about at the play and the invention of war and it will somewhat ease the tension.

Today, though, it is a real sortie. From offloads, the men on the boats have graduated to doing airdrops off the Bahamas. They fly loads of grass in from Jamaica through what is called the "Keys back country" to boats that have marked out a spot, and they will drop the dope to them. It is usually fairly simple. But not today. "You've got company. Air Force has scrambled. Head back," the radio man warns. Making a steep bank and diving low, the pilot heads back to Jamaica. The Air Force jets seek out their prey, but finding nothing, they return.

Chapter 4
Salad Days

Lynn and William Edward Wood were two or three years apart in age. They had gone to school together but really knew each other more by reputation and by overlapping circles of friends and because the Keys is a small pond. "Woody had two brothers. We all had hot rods and fooled around together," Lynn recalls. In time, they would combine their passions for aeronautics and boating into lucrative drug smuggling enterprises, but that would happen later and through their mutual friendship with Ricou Deshaw. The three of them got their start doing entry-level dope grunt work and marijuana was truly their gateway drug. "Ricou and I were actually smuggling long before Woody got in the game. He did like many guys in the Keys did and worked for somebody and then did his own trip." They all started on the periphery as off loaders, evolved to putting together their own dope deals and then post-graduated to dealing in cocaine. As their confidence, aspirations and sophistication grew, the number of trips grew, the more brazen they became. The trio would later collaborate on a few deals, but in the beginning they were spinning in separate orbits and pretty oblivious to each other.

Deshaw was Lynn's age, had grown up with him, was also ruggedly handsome and fit. The two of them had been best friends since the Sixth Grade. They played ball, fished, boated, hung out - all of the things guys do on the Keys. His father was a commercial airline pilot so Deshaw's life was a bit easier than Dickie's. But to them these class distinctions carried less weight. If Ricou got a new Z-28 Camaro, Dickie would just get an old one and soup it up to be just as bad a ride. After college, Ricou went to flight school and was "right seat" for a prestigious Lear Jet charter service. He started buying planes and he and Dickie would fly together. He taught Dickie how to fly. They bought the next plane together and started hot-rodding in the air. "It was fun."

"I've been smuggling dope all my life," Lynn says, acknowledging that he's no angel. He started around 1973, a short while after he quit high school. In the Keys it was an important cash crop and, he claims, everyone was in on it. All his peers, his high school coach, everyone. "I brought in a load of pot to my principal's house. The whole Keys, that's all they did. Even law enforcement was in on it." A friend's dad ran *bolita* up and down the Keys and was connected to the corruption and patronage system which permeates every level of the Conch Republic and what they call the "Bubba System."

Key West was getting too hot for them. They asked Dickie if he could lead a boat into the Upper Keys end of the island chain. Lynn knew the back country like the back of his hand and they wanted him to meet *The Billfisher*, a 55-foot commercial lobster boat built in Key West and guide their 5000-pound pot load to an isolated spot that he knew near the Cheeca Lodge resort. The Channel 5 bridge tender was paid $10,000. Dickie led them in. He and his friend went to the shore to wait for the boat, but it ran aground. They improvised, running the load to shore with only two small skiffs and working through the night to rid the boat of the contraband. The next day, the folks in Key West told Dickie that if he could get the boat off the sandbar it was his. He returned only to find a bevy of Coast Guard vessels there. "That's what I did. I was 19 years old and they gave me $35,000 cash. That was it. I was gone."

"The Cheeca Lodge was at one time called the Ollie Inn before Twitchell bought it. We actually based our early smuggling out of the property next door to Cheeca where my mom worked. It was a small beach house owned by a guy named Scutter (Scutter's Beach) and it's now called The Moorings. Twitchell actually owned a private island with a 7500-square-foot, ranch-style house on it, very private and secure. It was only used a couple of weeks in the winter months. We would put 75,000 pounds in it at a time and move it off the island in motor homes, campers, beer trucks, you name it." Some time later, Deshaw came home from college and was driving a dump truck. "I got him involved in smuggling pot with me and we became partners. We did our own little thing for a while and then I went to prison."

Ricou moved on, connecting with Woody (and Dickie's ex-wife). Deshaw had been a Miami Hurricanes football player and was a star of sorts. He even had a brush with the NFL where he is still the subject of an urban legend. Dickie got out of prison and started doing construction work. "When I first got out of prison for like a year we didn't speak. We'd pass each other on the road and he'd wave and I wouldn't wave. Finally at a party we made a peace agreement. He came out with a bottle of Jack Daniels and a couple of glasses and said 'Have a drink with me.' I said 'Go back inside. I don't want to drink with you.' He started crying and saying 'Everything I've done in my whole life I've done with you, hunting, fishing, everything.' We hugged and went back into the party. Everybody was happy for us. We started smuggling together."

Chapter 5
Getting It Together

Things had gone quite well for Woody, so well that it had made him filthy rich. Woody wanted more. He started talking about a friend with Colombian connections. "Frank says he has some connections back home. How do you feel about flying from Columbia?" Wood asked Deshaw. Woody, who had by now been doing this for a few years, set it out. One of them - they were all pilots - would fly to Columbia. "We fly back to Bahamas. Rock Sound. I've already checked out that strip. It's sweet. We'll use the same crew, same system, we're just changing commodities."

But now, there were even more moving parts and a much larger area of operation. On one of the Bahamas trips, the boat broke down. Ricou landed and immediately noticed the change of operations. The cargo was being offloaded into pickup trucks instead of being taken to the water. "We good?" he asked Woody. "No. We have a problem. The boat only made it to Bimini before it broke down. I flew a mechanic with a new engine and spare parts to fix it, but the captain quit." They were in a pickle, he explained.

"I have someone we can trust," Ricou offered. "He's been out of work 'cause of a boat accident. I'll pay him out of my share if I have to." "That's not necessary. Who is it?" "Dickie." Woody was dubious. "It's a pretty hard run. I know he knows the water around here but can he run a trip that far across the ocean?" Ricou was confident. "He can do it and he needs the money. How much will it pay, so I can tell him?" "$250,000."

"I had just gotten out of prison. I was doing construction work. I was out there sweating and pounding nails and pouring concrete," Lynn explains. Hell yes, he was in. The next day Dickie was fully engaged. "So, how's this going to work?" he asked. "The pickup boat is a 37-foot Midnight Express strapped with four 200-horsepower Mercury outboards.

You jump off the coast to Bimini and meet us at Rock Sound. Ricou and Kevin are picking up 700 keys in Columbia. That's somewhere about 50 duffle bags. The boat will have plenty of room but you'll need at least one crewman. Shouldn't take you more than an hour and then back out into the night. When you get to within three miles of our rendezvous point, you'll off load to the smaller boats who'll be waiting for you, probably Tavernier Key but maybe somewhere south of Miami. We stay in constant touch with the high frequency radios."

In Columbia, Deshaw and Kevin Sheehy landed in a sugarcane field and waited impatiently. From the opposite direction another aircraft landed, spun itself around, dumped the cocaine onto the ground and left immediately. Almost simultaneously, a truck arrived, threw more cocaine to the ground. Kevin and Ricou quickly loaded the cocaine and took off headed for Orange Walk, Belize to refuel. Over Belize, they frantically searched for the signal flares and the strip. "Orange Walk, I can't see you." The silence broke. "I hear you. You are south of me, look north." "I see you." They landed the plane on nothing more substantial than a road next to a sugar cane field. And just as briskly, the locals ran and refueled them. A man met the plane. "Carlos?" Ricou delivered him money in a paper sack and was surprised to receive one back. "What's in the bag?" Sheehy asked. They laughed. It was fried chicken. "Nice."

The three of them did a couple more deals and, while they did not officially part ways, they were doing their own things. Wood started dealing in coke and Dickie and Ricou started flying marijuana from Belize into Louisiana. Dickie had met Gary Young at the Eglin prison camp. "We were on the same work detail and he started telling me about a connection he had in Belize with Freddy Pou. I called him up and went up there." Young and Marks Bagalman, a Louisiana attorney, had access to a plane. Fred Hartley was one of their pilots. They went up to Louisiana to scout out his idea about flying a load from Belize and dropping it into the rivers near New Orleans and Lake Charles. "The Navajo that Gary used wasn't his or

Marks'. It belonged to some guy who had a Lube Shop or something like that. They were actually 'stealing' it and if anything happened to it they were going to report it stolen. The owner knew nothing about the trip to Belize. We actually dropped the loads in a tugboat channel right by Whiskey Bay and it was a straight canal over five to six miles long, perfect for air-drops."

Marks and Hartley met Ricou and Dickie on the apron at Lake Front Airport in New Orleans and headed to Lake Charles. With the coordinates keyed into the Loran, they dropped a test run Igloo cooler into the water. They were satisfied. This was going to be much easier than flying into the Bahamas and around Key West's defenses. The change in locale not only made them formalize organizational structures, it got them acquainted and appreciative of state-of-the-art planes and high-tech communications equipment. They flew to Chicago, took delivery of a new aircraft and headed home to South Florida to put this thing together.

They flew as teams, Fred and Marks and Ricou and Dickie. They would go to Orange Walk, Belize where they would meet with the load plane, follow it to a strip, transfer the dope, take off and return to Louisiana. Once home, they would make radio contact and head for the canal. When they saw the signals below - the flares, or whatever - the copilot would pop a glow stick, place it on a bundle and throw it out of the plane. Three runs over the canal and then back to the Big Easy.

But if making money doing something illegal and highly profitable was easy and not dangerous, everyone would do it. The business was full of headaches and stress. And danger. The Louisiana trips, too, had their own intrinsic sets of problems, not the least of which was the additional travel distance. During one of those trips, Fred and Marks radioed Lynn that they were just about out of fuel. "We better find a goddamn field pretty soon or I will have to head to Cancun. We are just about out of juice," he said, angrily explaining to Lynn just "why the fuck" he "could be out of fuel "This is a straight factory Navaho, dude. No mods, no extra fuel tanks, bladder, long-range nothing. We're just about dry," he snapped. Ricou and Dickie had flown down to Belize in the 404 Cessna they had just bought, formerly a Burger King corporate airplane that they referred to as "BK," the last two letters of its tail number. "Found it!" Lynn radioed. Fred could see Lynn's plane circling below and followed him down. They landed on a two-track road. The Navajo landed behind the Cessna. The planes, parked end to end, were loaded. They put 1200 pounds on the Navajo and 1600 pounds on the Cessna.

Marks was first out. They made it to Louisiana. They spotted the lights in the canals. "Butte LaRose, is that you?" "We're here, let her rip." The next morning Marks and Fred were eating breakfast up on St. Charles somewhere, congratulating themselves on just how big and how easy last night's score was when their partner Gary Young gave them the bad news. Actually, it was way past "bad" news. It was up somewhere around "horrendously horrible disaster" news. Dickie's 404 was wider than the Navajo. When they pulled it up at about 80 knots on the muddy ground the torque pulled them off into the trees. They were lucky to be alive. They torched the plane and headed home. "Right after you left, they slid off the airstrip. It was too muddy and the plane was too heavy from the load. They unloaded the shit and torched the plane." "They torched a 404 Titan?" Marks shouted. "Yeah, man, that's the cost of doing business. So is going back for the rest of the load," he shot back, and walked off.

That same day, Ricou and Dickie were trying to blend in as they passed through Customs at New Orleans International Airport. They had been in Belize on business, they told the customs inspector. "I'm a pilot." But the agent's suspicions darkened. They had purchased their plane tickets with cash and had bunches of cash on them. They had blank documents and other questionable paperwork in the briefcase. When he discovered a false bottom in Dickie's briefcase, even though it was empty, he pulled them aside and, eventually, to another office for a closer inspection. The contents of the briefcases were secretly copied and they were told that they were free to go.

Free to go, sure, but not free from suspicion. Customs and Enforcement Special Agent Arthur Wicks trailed them into the New Orleans Central Business District, down to Poydras and Magazine Streets. And if Ricou was an easy target to spot - big, handsome, obviously athletic white boy carrying a carved wooden Honduran sculpture - so, too, it must have been easy to spot the agent because they "made" him. They watched him from a hotel lobby and slipped away. It was time to book it for sure. Louisiana obviously wasn't working. The Bahamas had too many moving parts, boats broke down, it required large crews, cargo had to be transported at sea from one boat to another. And now, it looked like they were hot in Louisiana.

Chapter 6
Heart of Dixie

The boys reconnected with Woody. They had a grand new plan. "Why don't we fly the stuff into Alabama? We have a camp up there and we have a fellow who knows about a couple of airstrips with nothing around it."" Fly straight into the country?" "Sure," they assured Woody. "There aren't any cops to speak of up there. No military. Not much of anything. We fly up over the Mexican peninsula, enter the US just west of New Orleans, cross around north of New Orleans and fly into what's basically Demopolis."

And radar? They had a connection in Customs who knew the weak spots. "About 125 miles offshore, we drop down to about a hundred to 200 feet and slow down to about 120 kilometers and mingle in with the helicopters that fly out of the oil rigs. No lights, in case of visuals." Easy. From Belize, the planes would mimic the breezes that meander into the expansive Gulf of Mexico. Hugging the surface, they would start their real seduction at the country's underbelly, Mobile Bay; working their way up her sultry tropical delta of river confluences, they would overfly the abandoned confederate dead at Blakely, look for the nearby landmark that is the aimless floating grey knot, the mangle of hundreds of moth-balled World War II battleships - the Ghost Fleet - that is tethered there on the Tensaw River and then follow the Tombigbee, ascending into the promise of her heights.

The country begins its elevation pyramid here. It rises, almost imperceptibly. From the wire grass in Dothan and the beaches in Mobile and Baldwin counties, it starts a noticeable bulge in Montgomery and gets real at around Birmingham. The interstate system divides the state into large pie-shaped sections. If you want to get anywhere in the *Heart of Dixie* that isn't on the interstate, you have to "go surface" on roads that are the roads of a very poor state; a 100-percent homegrown, blue-collar, mostly rural, Red State. It has two, essentially major, urban cities but it is a place mostly of camps and trailers, satellite dishes, convenience stores, railroad crossings, and redundantly-named primitive Baptist churches. It's all about, in order of importance, football, God, drinking, NASCAR, hunting and fishing. It is blessed with beautiful natural resources like the sugar-white beaches of the Gulf of Mexico. But, primarily, it is thousands of acres of pristine woods and national forests, great hunting seasons, plenty of deer, turkey and all other sorts of game.

One seeks diversions and entertainment here like one pans for gold, looking for it avidly and rejoicing in the accident of its discovery. It could be a beautiful river scene with a Vermont-like covered bridge on an old country road. Or boating at night on the Tennessee River, the majestic serenity punctuated by the croaking of millions of frogs, a nuclear power plant its austere backdrop. It could be the view from Cheaha or Lake Martin or riding horses in the Talladega National Forest.

It could even be the Zen slap of running across the quirky rustic theme park some farmer has created out of hay bales and found objects in literally the middle of nowhere at Forkland. With not much more than an enigmatic driftwood sign of the family name over the portal and a Latin exhortation, *acta non verba*, these little vignettes sit out here like some sort of Amish version of Disneyland. A tin man guards. A leprechaun chortles. A boat sails on a sea of these huge rolls of hay. Dinosaurs lurk. A covered wagon heads west. A Trans-AM rides high on slicks of dry grass. And, ironically, a Snoopy chases the Red Baron.

Dickie, Ricou, and Curtis Turpin, too, believe in "actions - not words." They have purchased LTD, a pretty nice backwoods hunting camp that sits nearby. The locals know the 200-hundred acre hunting club as "Felix Larkin's Old Place." Pretty near the Gulf-State's paper mill and almost on Paul Reed Swamp it wasn't too far from Sparky's Grocery story and about a mile away from the Demopolis Airport. The Tombigbee River meanders nearby on its way to Mobile Bay where it will merge with its other big brothers to form the Mobile Bay Delta and up which they will fly. The guys had been bringing their friends, some of them professional football players, up here to do "green field deer hunting" but now they planned to move their base of operations here.

The closest city to the camp was to the south, in bordering Marengo County at Demopolis, a city that sits dead center in the sylvan void created by the interstates that are its boundaries. Bypassed, likewise, by economic development and history, the area is named for the richness of its soil and, therefore, the ability to grow what was once the South's "king" crop. More than a few have found either irony or intention in the Black Belt's demographics. It is predominantly Black and poor. Hunting camps, large timber tracts, ancestral homes and a few scattered families are just about the only thing here. Not much happens here and the only real reason for non-locals to come through here is that they are on the way to the University of Alabama in Tuscaloosa or because it serves as a shortcut to some Mississippi town. That was the beauty it held for the boys.

Woody didn't turn it down outright. He wanted to peep it. So they flew up to Alabama where they were met by a local who took them out to the field. They measured it. They walked the grounds. They scouted the area from the air. The hunting camp was perfect and Ricou sold Woody on the idea. "The camp is around on the other side of the river, only about a mile from the airport. It's kind of curvy, cause of the river but this gives us access to the two airstrips." Ricou gave him the rest of the skinny. "We unload off the truck and put it into the cooler. After we store the shit and the rest of the guys return with the generators and the other field equipment, we load the cars to get out and put the equipment in the cooler so it doesn't get ripped off," Ricou explained. "After the guys leave with the load, the plane comes in, picks us up and we're back home sipping Mojitos before you know it."

"What about Belize? One of us has to handle that. That leaves us short a pilot." Ricou suggested their lawyer in New Orleans. "He's a pilot, has flown some trips for us." "A fucking lawyer? No way! I don't trust those fuckers, certainly not with a monster load of cocaine," Woody screamed. "If we decide to do this, I'll fly with Fred. Ricou you do Belize and Dickie you handle the Alabama operation."

Chapter 7

Freedom Fighters

Celestino Mendez moves in the anonymous shadows of the condemned and must now feel that he has come full circle. Except that where once he was the indomitable, the proud, the erect, the formidable thorn, the implacable foe of what he might rightfully think of as tyranny, he is now legitimately that very "worm," the *gusano*, so vilified by his most mortal of enemies. His well-earned and deserved ignominy and dishonor has even stripped him of his name, a mechanism fashioned as protection from the prospect of revenge for his ultimate perfidy. He has committed the mortal sin of men of combat, the betrayal of one's comrades, of his benefactor country and of the old world code of honor.

Mendez, or whatever they are calling him now, is shuffled around the federal prison system under an assumed identity provided by the Federal Witness Protection Program. He is doing a 20-year sentence, a bargain considering his multi-jurisdictional, multi-count drug distribution charges. But it is a good deal at a great cost. It is for him that a United States Attorney from Miami has traveled to Bangor, Maine to plead for what he characterized as "one of the most important witnesses for the government to come before the court," no small assessment coming from a Miami prosecutor. Mendez is the thread that unravels the cloth that lays bare the emperor's nude state and leads to the collapse of more than one drug empire. And it would begin with a friendship from the old country.

In Havana, Sylvia Alvarez has watched more than her fair share of Castro's speeches and is, today, just as conflicted as the Det 1 airman. She is no foe of the revolution, but as a middle-aged member of the Cuban middle class she is getting wobbly. Now a retired functionary, she runs a *casa particular*, a private home that rents rooms to visitors under government supervision. It helps her pay their bills. She is annoyed to still be centered on scrounging for essentials and scoring "luxuries" like an extra-special dinner once a week. "In Cuba, everyone has a scam. If you don't, you don't survive."

Her husband Miguel, works as a Cuban Television technician. They are both educated and live comfortable lives. Their Art Nouveau Apartment building faces the Ministry of the Interior and once housed a large United States corporation before the government expropriated it. From her balcony you can see the famous boulevard La Rampa and the Hotel Nacional, the Malecón sea wall and the tribute to the Battleship Maine. Less than a mile beyond the memorial is the American Interests Section, which still hasn't responded to her requests to allow her to visit friends in the states.

In Miami this "condo" would be out of reach for someone of their class. Yet, she is pissed. They have struggled through the Revolution, the "Special Period" and *cada otra pendejada* and it just never seems to end. Her universe is now much more introverted and introspective. Her collective consists of her immediate family, her friends and the other tenants in her building; like Lourdes and her two young girls who she protects from falling into *jineterismo* or the elderly lady on the third floor about whom she is ever mindful because she is so frail and alone and because Sylvia is Cuban and, thus, characteristically charitable and generous.

Too young to have taken an active part in any actual fighting, Sylvia was excited when, one year "After the Triumph of the Revolution" Fidel announced *la Campaña Nacional de Alfabetización en Cuba*, a bold plan to heighten the country's literacy rate. Visiting the United Nations, the characteristically audacious Fidel had shared with the world his ambitious plan to send 100,000 children, aged twelve and above, along with more than a quarter million volunteer teachers, into the countryside to teach the *campesinos* to read. Her standard issue grey uniform could not mask the pride she felt, the joy at being given the opportunity to serve her country at such a young age. Buoyed by the naivety of the youthfulness that she now shared with her country, she set off. "*Yo sí puedo,*" she cried, repeating the theme of the campaign.

Armed with her zeal and the *brigadista's* standard issue - a warm blanket, a hammock, two textbooks - she worked by day alongside her host family. At night, under the light of the gas-powered lantern she had been provided, she set out to make her country a proud place. She marched gleefully into the future. Thirty-five years later she hardly thinks about it. When she does she speaks of it as her proudest moment but has some unkind words to say about the *alzados*, the counter-revolutionaries that she characterizes as terrorists and murderers.

She had felt a combination of fear and exhilaration in serving her country at such a young age. Sylvia had marched into a history so much bigger than even she imagined. As part of a movement now named for the first of what would become many martyrs, she would bravely face a campaign of counter-revolution, intimidation, violence, and international intrigue. Only a few months after Castro declared his bold plan of bringing literacy to the country, a young teacher was executed by the *alzados*. It only served to bring that much more heat to the passions of a country now energized by revolution. The members of the literacy campaign were now called the Conrado Benitez Brigade and, she'll tell you proudly, she was one of them.

One man's terrorist is another's freedom fighter. The CIA made common cause with the opposition, cooking up schemes to destabilize the country. Given the go-ahead, they put into motion a series of campaigns that would lend aid and comfort to the enemies of the new Cuban government. Clandestine flights from the United States dropped supplies to the many homegrown enemies of the Cuban regime who served as our cover for the dirty work of disrupting the Cuban economy. Whatever their label, they would be accused of burning farms, stores and utilities, of killing soldiers, peasants and *brigadistas* like Sylvia and of causing disruptions and discontent for the fledgling government.

Fernando Pruna was one of those insurgents. The son of a prominent Havana lawyer, he earned an advanced Economics degree in the United States and worked here. In 1957, he returned to Cuba and was soon elected to their House of Representatives. A member of the opposition *Movimiento de Recuperación Democrática* (MRD), he was arrested in 1959 and sentenced to 20 years in prison. But he escaped and joined the resistance movement, fighting in the mountains of the Escambray. He was recaptured and, along with two major CIA operatives, was accused of numerous acts of "banditry" and murder. At the age of 24, a Cuban revolutionary tribunal sentenced him to death.

At the same time that Sylvia and her other young comrades waged war on illiteracy, these covert actions blossomed into an open war. In *Against All Hope*, Armando Valladares' remarkable homage to the human spirit, he mentions seeing the Bay of Pigs invasion from his window in the Isle of Pines where he, Celestino Mendez and Fernando Pruna were incarcerated. On that beach was Pruna's brother Andres, valiantly engaged in battle. The younger Pruna had joined *Brigada 2506* that January. An aspiring artist, he had been pushed by events to join the resistance. Because he had been a champion swimmer, he volunteered to be part of the invasion's Underwater Demolition Team (UDT). They had been training for months under the supervision of the CIA, had sailed from Miami, had gone to Vieques, an island off of the coast of Puerto Rico, and then on to New Orleans. From there they joined the Cuban Expeditionary Force invasion fleet as "Operation Pluto" was set in motion.

Alighting from their mother ship just before midnight of April 16, 1961 were the eleven frogmen. They were divided into three teams, one of them led by Pruna, who was by now packing a BAR and all the bravado that can possibly be packed into his lithe 19-year-old swimmer's physique. They were missioned with the duty of preparing the beach for the invasion and would hit at three entry points, code-named Blue Beach, Red Beach and Green Beach and they were the vanguard of an invasion force of nearly

1,500 men. Pruna's team, charged with hitting Playa Larga (Red Beach), boarded one of the two catamarans that had been outfitted with .50 and .30 machine guns. The UDT would be the first to fire shots in this three-day war.

History informs us that the effort was a fiasco. The United States withdrew its support from the world's worst-kept secret. The planning had gone all haywire, the counter-revolution was birthed but stillborn. The invasion became a military and political blunder of international proportions. And while other frogmen would be among the captured and dead of those few nights, not Pruna. He escaped the debacle and was by all accounts a heroic actor. His team accomplished their mission, hitting the beach and marking it for the troop landing, but only after engaging in a fire fight to get in and another on the way out. Safely on board, he even returned days later on a suicide mission to rescue other fighters who had been stranded on the beach. Upon his return to Miami he was given a hero's welcome as well as a commission in the United States Navy.

There is a remarkable misconception about Castro who is often portrayed as just a maniacal anomaly. For better and worse, though, Castro is really your typical Cuban. They are a brilliant, quick, courageous, gracious, dogmatic, principled, and vibrant people who are often driven by these qualities to extremes and their resultant contradictions. During the first days of his administration, it had been the indefatigable nature of the Cubans that would push Kennedy, a newly-elected President who now found himself heir to a fully-hatched invasion plan, to view what was being termed his "disposal problem." If the invasion were called off, he was warned, it could have political ramifications or, worse yet, the Cubans were armed and in Guatemala. They might choose to fight there. His Machiavellian response was that "If we have to get rid of these men, it is much better to dump them in Cuba than in the United States, especially if that is where they want to go." (Years later, Castro would use this tactic when he dumped his mentally ill and criminals into the Mariel boat lift.)

One of the more common traits of a Cuban is utter and dogged stubbornness. At the prison camp, Valladares, Celestino Mendez, and Fernando Pruna, remained ever defiant. Even in captivity they were locked in a petulant battle of wills with their jailers. For every action, however, there was an equally stubborn reaction and in the process they bore the full rage of a cruel penal machinery. So much so that their doggedness drew attention beyond the walls of their enslavement and the *plantados*, as they would come to be called, became another steely symbol of resistance to the Cuban regime itself. They were routinely beaten and tortured, suffered horrific depravities, and witnessed the savage murders of their compatriots.

The authorities initiated a campaign of "rehabilitation." The minor concession of wearing the special uniforms issued to the compliant would ensure better treatment and privileges. The *plantados* refused to capitulate. They planned and executed escapes. When caught, they were punished in ways that can bear no real justification. They persisted. Fernando somehow had his death sentence commuted to 35 years. By 1978 he had apparently become "rehabilitated." He was wearing the uniform and saying the things his captors wanted to hear. He was released in 1980 after having served 17 years and returned to Miami.

Rehabilitated? Less than a year after Fernando's reentry into the United States, a federal indictment alleged, the Pruna brothers had begun distributing major quantities of dope. Celestino Mendez, who had been caught in Maine, had ratted them out. It was an unraveling daisy-chain and their connection to Wood would lead to Dickie and others.

Chapter 8

The Hartley Boys

About a year and a half after the razing of the 404 Titan in Belize, Demopolis Police Department Sergeant Robert Meigs responded to a call about a plane crash at a nearby field. The small plane's wreckage was strung across the field, the pilot's badly burned body still smoldered on the tarmac where it lay. Small packages were scattered about. Their entrails lisped little white clouds of fine powder that coupled with the haze of the smoke and the morning mist and wafted off into the sultry Alabama morning. It was a narcotics scene uncommon for this small town. Helicopters buzzed overhead. Crime investigation vehicles were scattered about. Techs and cops were everywhere.

A conga line of Alabama State Trooper cars descended. Meigs knew Trooper Sergeant Ed Odom. If the boys from Miami met all of the Hollywood Central casting qualities for *Miami Vice*, Ed Odom surely qualified for a role as a redneck Sheriff in *Mississippi Burning*. Born and bred in the rough and tumble part of south Mobile County, he is a tobacco-chewing, no nonsense, brusque, plain-talking big bear of a man with a matching *basso profundo* voice. He was at the scene in what was his standard working attire, K-mart jeans, work shirt, shit-kicker boots and Trooper cowboy hat. Meigs filled him in.

"The airplane is in three parts. Looks like they went through the ditch and landed in the road. There's a burned body laying on the edge of the pavement 10 to 15 feet from the main fuselage area, another one inside and a lot of packages, probably cocaine, spread out over the ground; some of it's partially burned and some completely burned up." "Any signs of others?" Odom asked. "Someone was waiting on them. Used a vehicle to break out the gate. Left some paint scrapes. We'll send it to Montgomery for analysis. Probably about 200 keys of cocaine. Paperwork looks like the plane is out of New Orleans." Odom pondered what he was being told. His tobacco chew underscored this rumination. "Hmmm." He left, offering to check back in a few days to see what else they had but he was starting to put some other pieces together.

Flying requires fearlessness and the art of drug smuggling is at its ceiling. Pilots, like lawyers, doctors or anyone else with highly specialized skill or training, have a tendency towards arrogance, not just towards others but as it relates to the dangers inherent in what they do. At first it didn't matter. Woody, Ricou and Dickie were pilots and friends. They were not afraid to get their hands dirty, worked well together and looked out for each other. It was an easy fit and a hell of a luxury, a working equilibrium with folks who were both crazy enough to engage in this behavior but were dependable too. Whether they worked for others or for themselves, they considered themselves working partners. Each of them had proven their reliability and loyalties.

Despite Woody's initial misgivings about Dickie's ability to pilot the boat, Lynn had come through with flying colors. "We hit 25 to 30 foot seas and almost didn't make it. Then when we got to Tavernier Key there was nobody there to meet us. They didn't think we would've come in with 40 mile per hour winds." When Woody got popped in St. Pete, it was Dickie that came up with the bread for his lawyer. Lynn, although not then involved, had even given Clark $30,000 so he could hire a lawyer. (Both of them would soon betray him.) Stuck in the boonies in Jamaica with a lot of locals gunning for you? Trust Ricou to not abandon you.

But Woody was gone after the first Alabama trip and Ricou would soon follow after only two or three trips. Frightened by a National Guard Black Hawk overflight, he just quit. Dickie found himself in the difficult posture of bringing in others and it wasn't always seamless. Dickie had met Fred Hartley during the Louisiana smuggling venture and they had continued working together even when Marks fell out of the picture. Fred almost immediately replaced Ricou as Dickie's full partner in crime and best friend.

The pilots were the lynchpins of this operation and a constant source of problems. It would start with Fred and Marks' abandonment of the Waynesboro load, begin to unravel with the plane crash and end with Clark's hijinks and ultimate betrayal. But there was a lot of angst along the way as they sought to find reliable replacements. Too often the new pilots were selfish and narcissistic when what the operation needed was unit cohesion. This was not so much the group of friends from the Keys but reckless mercenaries looking for a quick buck and a quicker turnaround.

The problems, according to Dickie, began almost immediately while they were still working in the Keys. A corrupt law enforcement agent had introduced them to Andy Pruna and they started doing drops with him. Pruna's pilot, Lynn said, "came over us so high that when the duffle bags hit the water they exploded. Plus, we would shine our spotlights straight up and he was supposed to start dropping when he passed the first boat and stop before he came too close to the second boat. He flew right over us and the bags were slamming all around us in the pitch black night." They worked around the exploding cargo problem. "We started using polyurethane foam to keep them from exploding and they were hard as a rock and very durable. You could drop them from 1000 feet if you wanted."

The very first trip, Woody and Fred flew 541 kilos to the clandestine strip that they were now calling "The Swamp." It worked wonderfully, Lynn said. But Griste cut Woody out almost immediately. "Bill said, 'Look, you guys are doing all of the work and it's your equipment and your spot. Why don't you work directly with me and my partners?'" They did a couple of more trips at "The Swamp," evolving their system as they went along. "Those first five or six trips were piece-mealed. It was a laundry list of owners, all with different marks and stamps on the kilos. They would load the plane until you couldn't cram another duffel bag in it. After the Waynesboro fiasco, we decided to keep loads to 600 kilos. Fred almost crashed two or three times in Belize from being over gross and the strip was wet and sloppy."

They had moved over to Demopolis after the second or third trip because of a near crash. Fred had hit some trees in Belize. "I had warned them that the plane they were using wasn't good for smuggling. It had all sorts of issues, like a pressurized cabin. But they went anyway." Miraculously, the trees only flexed and catapulted the aircraft back into the air, allowing him to recover and land. But the gear was bent and Fred had to cycle it three or four times to get it up. He would not make it home with his gear down. He was about to turn around and go back when it finally cycled. When he landed in Alabama the leading edges of the wings were all dented up and now they were afraid to cycle the gear again. They hopped the plane over to the airfield at Demopolis." Noone came to investigate. The field was mostly inactive. The next morning they flew the plane to Miami for repairs and started thinking about the field. "It seemed like a great spot. Why spend all that time putting out lights and landing on the grass in the woods? We had the perfect place and it even had a rotating beacon for the wayward pilot to find."

Dickie and Fred had done about six or eight trips with Griste when, as Valdes tells it in his book *Coming Clean*, the partnership began to show "signs of stress." The stressor, according to Lynn, was because "Bill tells me 'You've been working with me and my partners and I think it's time you meet them since you already know one of them.'" They had their meeting and one of the partners turned out to be Jorge Valdes, a Cuban expatriate who Dickie knew from his incarceration at Eglin. The other was Ismael Meza, a Columbian. "They claimed they needed to pay for the 714 kilos that were lost in Waynesboro but that they would make it up to us. So Fred and I paid $535,000 as our half of the loss." Dickie usually kept part of the load as security for his payment. Griste convinced them to release it all. That was the last they heard from them. They not only lost the load, they had to pay their crew out of their pocket. "They just ripped us off," Fred said angrily. "I told him, 'We don't need them. They needed us. Let's just move on and chalk this up to experience.'" They already had the connections to Andy. "We went ahead and started doing our own thing."

Now back with Pruna, the pilot resurfaced as a problem. He was reckless and refused to stay with the game plan. He crashed a 404 Cessna in Belize. Dickie complained to Andy that a conscientious pilot would have personally inspected the strip, would have seen that the extra thousand feet of runway was just "rough run-off" meant only as an extra buffer for takeoffs and not meant for landings. The nose gear folded like an accordion. An expensive plane laden with millions of dollars of cargo lay in ruins. Bagalman, who along with Hartley went back to Belize to finish the load, described the plane as "nestled back in the weeds covered up and couldn't get out of the strip there with all that weight."

That was soon followed by more problems. "We had let Andy land on 'Miss Lisa,' our strip in Belize. Andy's pilot could not take back off. He made three or four attempts but didn't have the *cojones* to make it out. Fred and Marks went down to Mexico picked up the load and blasted right out in 3200' and he had to stand there and watch. They came straight to Demopolis where I unloaded them. Piece of cake." Meanwhile, the other pilot was sent back to Colombia to pick up another load in a 404 Titan. This time he by-passed Belize and came straight to Demopolis. "He was supposed to land as quietly as possible and we would unload it and he could start up and leave in about 5 minutes. Being the complete coward he was, he spun it around at the end of the runway and kept it revved up while his copilot threw out the duffel bags. Then he turned all his lights on and roared off. This put all of my guys in jeopardy since it was not only loud as hell but the guys who worked at the chlorine plant were standing out in the front watching him take off. That was his one and only trip to Demopolis."

"After a few more trips with me going it alone, Fred and I agreed to be partners. He would do all the flying and take care of the planes, *et cetera*, and I'd handle Alabama and the trip back to Miami. We had done several trips when Ricou came over to my house just as I was heading out the door for Alabama and he said 'Where you going?' and I told him Fred was already on his way south and he said 'Let me run home and grab some clothes and I'll go with you.' I said 'Well, Fred and I are partners now so that might cause some problems' and he just went back home. That was it. He never worked again."

Strawberry blonde and light-complected, Hartley spoke with the trademark Flatbush accent of the Louisiana Cajun but he was not your typical bayou swamp rat. He had the complete corporate pilot package. Outgoing, stylishly dressed and immaculately groomed, he was as at home on the Louisiana woods as he was in the Big Easy board rooms. He could dance Zydeco in Lafayette and Ballroom Dance in New Orleans. "I bought him a California-made ski boat that would do about 90 miles per hour because he told me he was getting blown away down in the bayou by all the locals. I went up to teach him all the in-and-outs of driving and being safe in it. He had already bought matching mag wheels for the trailer and his truck. We took my wife and his girlfriend down into the bayous and all the locals were rafted up on a little sand island and we drove by real slow and they all ran and jumped in their 'speed' boats and came after us. Needless to say we let them catch up and then walked away from them like they had their anchors out. He was grinning ear-to-ear and then we went back to the sand bar and all the Cajuns came up to admire his new toy."

"I'm not sure of who he used to fly for but it was with different corporation planes. He might have just taken jobs that came along for all I know because he didn't have a steady job when we first got hooked up. We actually met through Marks and Gary Young. Fred knew absolutely nothing about smuggling but sure knew how to fly. When I say smooth I'm talking about his technique for taking off and landings. When you cannot feel the wheels leave the ground or touch down on landing, it's smooth and he was the best at that, God bless him. When I would sit at the end of the runway at Demopolis all you would hear was two little chirps and he'd come rolling up to the end almost silent. Pablo (Escobar) called him *Perfecto* and really liked him, probably for his success as much as his ability." On September 25, 1987, though, Fred Earl Hartley's perfect skills were lacking, his lucky steak had run its course. On his approach to the airport at Demopolis, Alabama, he clipped the top of a pine tree and crashed, killing himself and his brother, Joseph Ray Hartley.

Chapter 9
Vaiden Field

It was nearly Christmas 1988 and not much was happening, especially in Marion, Alabama. Unless you're Steve Purvis. It had been a little over a year since the crash and here they were giving it another go. Hartley's death didn't slow them down. Not even when Kevin Sheehy got busted over at Purvis' nearby camp. They just switched to Vaiden Field, one of the alternate landing strips less than 50 miles away. Purvis, too, was from the Keys and a childhood friend of Dickie and Ricou's. His job was to meet the plane, help unload the duffel bags and refuel. The pilot, Bob Clark, had been overseeing the operation when he heard the perimeter lookout warn. "We have company!" Purvis looked up and spotted the three cop cars bearing down on the field. Clark jumped back into the plane. He slammed his hands across the switches, deftly awakening the beast with his one ninja move. The other man was now in the copilot's seat. The pilot gave it full throttle. The aircraft jumped forward, fish-tailing into a perfect takeoff position. Off they went without much more of a discussion or warning than Clark's assertion that "I can make it."

At another part of the field the lookout watched as more cop cars arrived. Two of them actually stationed themselves at his position. They were so close he could hear them talking with each other and could hear the chatter over the radios. He was frozen. He reached down and, just in case one of his guys called, turned his hand-held off. He was oh so very still for what seemed forever. At long last, when a pickup truck - bar lights and loud muffler - joined the other two cop cars, he made cover and slipped away. Back at the field, Purvis had taken the nozzle out of the fuel tank. He signaled Clark and when it was obvious that the lunatic pilot intended to take off, he booked it out of there. Purvis, now in the pickup truck, watched the game of chicken, watched the cops chase the plane, saw the plane lift off, saw the cops coming after him, and drove his vehicle into the woods as "far as that mother fucker would go."

Marion Police Department Chief of Police John Anderson was at the end of the field. The radio call came in. "The plane is taking off." "I can see that! What else do you see?" "Tail lights." He ordered his officers to go check it out and held his position at the entrance. Shortly, Odom's cruiser pulled up to what was by now a hectic scene reminiscent of the other: bloodhounds, cop cars, and evidence units. A Black Hawk helicopter flew overhead. Anderson ran it down for Odom. "We got a call last night from someone at the field, said there was some suspicious activity. It was cold, wet and misty. Some rain. My guys rode in hot just as I had pulled up to the gate. The plane went at them. Damndest thing. Cowboy took off right over them, doused his lights and disappeared. Not much of an ID on the plane, long nose. I don't know much about aircraft. I was at the gate as he came off the end of the strip. Part of the time it was lit and part of the time it wasn't. He turned his lights off. The plane had spotlights, sort of, on the wings. He came off the airstrip and bore to the right, went dark and disappeared. We have the pilot's paperwork."

Odom, inspected the paperwork and told Anderson that they were looking for a Cessna 404. "Any dope?" "No dope. But we chased the pickup truck into the woods, an S-10, Florida plates. Got stuck in the mud. Awful lot of crap inside. Maps, lighting equipment, batteries. There's a fuel drum and an electric pump in the bed. Battery with some sort of electrical hookup, a set of lights in a Pampers box, walkie-talkies, and a rifle. Looks like at least two people fled from here." "Oh trust me, there's more than two. Get Customs and see if we can get some of their aircraft with the heat-seekers up here from Mobile. These guys aren't virgins. We've wasted too much time on these fuckers. How about tracks?" "No, the mud is like quicksand. Nothing there but holes where their shoes went in. You pull your foot out and all you get for an impression is a pool of goo. Makes it hard for our boys to run, though."

Hidden in the darkness of the field's periphery and now alone, one of the lookouts had watched it all go down. He had slipped away from his position and now was stuck in who knows where with the horrible too-late realization that it's a hell of a long way back to the Keys. He was struggling to maintain and on top of that his fat ass was having a rough go of it in this god awful terrain. You didn't run in this soup. Every step required pulling your boot out of some sticky muck. He radioed frantically. "Home plate"? "Sparrow"? "This is 'Side Door'. Come in." No answer. And, then, just when he thought it couldn't get any worse, the night became ever so more frightening. A huge helicopter - A FUCKING HELICOPTER - was flying overhead and shining a spotlight as bright as the sun. He wasn't going to make it.

At the camp, too, there was panic. "Home plate" had radioed, telling them that everyone was on their own. "We're out of here. We'll see you tomorrow." At the camp, two others frantically rummaged through the bunkhouse looking for keys to the only vehicle left there. Having finally found the keys to the van, they were on their way out when they heard "Side Door's" May Day. "This is Sparrow, we're at base. Coming to you. Head for Highways 80 and 5."

The next morning, Odom was still at Vaiden Field when he got a "hit" on his BOLO (Be On Look Out). Alabama State Trooper Bobby Brown radioed from Muscle Shoals with the news that a plane fitting the description had landed there that night. "Look in the plane's manual and let me know if page 45 is missing and keep me posted." Brown had been checking the local hotels, but he seemed to be always just a few steps behind these guys. He kept at it. "They just checked out and called for a cab for the airport," he was told. And, finally, he found them at the Muscle Shoals airport terminal. He confronted one of them. "Tim Weaver?"

Brown reported back to Odom. "Got two suspects with tickets to Tampa. Bought tickets in the name of Tim Weaver and Bob McCoy. Turns out their real names are Patrick Abbott and Robert Clark. They're denying everything. By the way, page 45 is missing in the manual." Odom assessed the situation. No dope. He directed Brown to squeeze the two of them for a while, collect information, IDs, fingerprints, and photographs and let them go. "Make sure we can find them when we need them," an exasperated Odom tells him. "Dammit," he exhaled, nearly imperceptibly.

Odom's exasperation is hard to understand. If the piney woods and its isolation is a tempting place to do drug smuggling, the Southern and Northern Districts of Alabama are horrible places to be a defendant. The mess smoldering at Demopolis had been a metaphor and Odom was well on his way to putting together the pieces. Multiple jurisdictions had started comparing notes and sharing information. The agents were unraveling the threads of a major tapestry of crime. But it was more like a Gordian Knot; Lynn was connected to Wood who was connected to Pruna and others and they, also, to others. But their luck was nearing its run. Wood would soon face indictments in multiple districts and bring the others down with him. To be sure, their activities were cross-pollinated by history, personnel, and friendships but it was really two pieces of a lot of moving parts. When Dickie and Ricou moved their operations to Louisiana and then Alabama, Wood had been only briefly involved and went on to do his own thing. It would take the agents, often working on the pieces of the puzzle independently, some time to figure that out. Dickie and his friends had actually been under the scope as far back as the stop at the New Orleans airport. During one of their trips, the fog had been too heavy and the pilots had headed back to New Orleans. They spotted a field in Mississippi and ditched the load there only to have it immediately discovered. Law enforcement started looking there.

In late 1984, Bagalman, their New Orleans lawyer and pilot, had put together a corporation that took delivery of one of the involved planes. Not even one year later Hartley, Bagalman, Deshaw, and Lynn flew to Chicago to buy another plane. The following month Dickie and Ricou bought one of the planes from Bagalman as a replacement for the plane they had torched in Belize. Customs had been watching another trafficker when it received a report that Dickie's aircraft had been spotted offloading duffel bags in Meridian, Mississippi. They opened an investigation there. Odom had started putting things into focus at about the time of the Waynesboro drop. The crash was the catalyst. Wicks had reported the Titan destroyed not more than 24 hours after they torched it in Belize; that's how closely they were being watched. These guys were toast, they just didn't know it.

Chapter 10
Stephen Bishop

Businessman Stephen Bishop arrived that bright sun-shiny morning at the St. Petersburg-Clearwater Airport. It was his intention to take delivery of his new aircraft and fly it home but it would not go as planned. Here, in the inner sanctum of the salesman's office where he had gone to finalize the million dollar sale, he received a shock. "William Wood, you're under arrest for conspiracy to falsely register an aircraft. You have a right to remain silent..." He was arrested by United States Customs and taken away for an initial appearance in Tampa's federal court. It would be his last taste of freedom for years.

A month before Wood's arrest, Michael Stanton, a small time cocaine smuggler had been arrested in Missouri. Afraid of getting busted, he asked his son and another boy to hide his stash. Stanton later retrieved the backpack and delivered it to Wood, who claimed that some of the cocaine was missing. Stanton, arrested for threatening the kids, started cooperating and gave up Wood. The arrest at the St. Pete airport was just a reason to hold him and more fuel for the fodder. The next day, a grand jury in St. Louis, Missouri indicted Wood for Conspiracy to Possess with the Intention to Distribute Drugs. Within four months, thanks to his federal speedy trial "rights," Wood had been tried, convicted, and sentenced to 20 years.

Eager to help her husband with his problems, Carol Wood merely made them worse. She contacted congressional aide Michael Smith and not less than three months after her husband's sentence, Carol made the first of seven bribes totaling $1.4 million to help derail the investigations. But "Smith" was really United States Customs Special Agent Mike Miller and the government now had what it characterized as the largest federal bribery sting in history. It also may have been the easiest to craft. The targets, according to federal officials, had more cash than curiosity. The news media portrayals of the effort painted them as pathetic rubes. "Neither of the supposed congressional aides ever told their guileless benefactors whom they worked for or exactly how they could block the investigations," one reporter noted.

Frank Basso, a Wood associate, was also on tape trying to make a bribe on his behalf and Wood even wrote a letter from the penitentiary in Ashland, Kentucky that implicated himself in the effort. Ten months after his sentence, Wood, who had been recorded orchestrating the effort with his wife from his cell at the federal penitentiary, was charged with paying bribes to obstruct grand jury investigations of drug smuggling and money laundering in Tampa, Mobile, Detroit and St. Louis and it was a solid case. An indictment named him, his wife Carol, Basso and David Carlson. Soon after, Metro-Dade Police Sergeant Perry Carrell, Carol's brother, was relieved of duty when federal drug agents found a receipt for a bank safety deposit box which, as it turned out, contained nearly half a million dollars and four Rolex watches. The entire Wood group rolled.

Agents traveled to Ashland to debrief Wood who had begun to cooperate. He gave up his inner circle, which included his brother-in-law Howard Carrell. Carrell fell. He began to cooperate and identified Christian Schmidgall as the radio operator for the marijuana airdrops in Florida. And, he gave details of an Alabama importation. Wood had left that part out. Agents from Florida and Alabama returned to interview Wood, this time with a "no more bullshit" warning. Wood was now more forthcoming. The 60-hour debriefing lasted nearly a week and yielded a 31-page report. He had not only implicated Schmidgall and Purvis, he detailed how things were done. He gave them a complete historical and logistical schematic. Two of his Columbian connections, he told them, were Fabio Ochoa and Pablo Escobar. The agents really got excited.

Wood told the agents how he and Ochoa had started importing cocaine into South Florida, explaining how they'd fly it from Colombia through Abaco Island in the Bahamas. They used anything that would suit their purpose - aircraft, boats, and trucks - to import and distribute the cocaine and move incredibly large sums of money back to the Bahamas. The cocaine was loaded onto "go fast" boats and smuggled into the Tavernier or Davis Reef areas of Key Largo, Florida. Smaller boats would meet the incoming boats and transport the cocaine to trucks waiting on shore. Those trucks were driven to Miami where the cocaine was further distributed. They would also airdrop large amounts of cash at Marsh Harbour.

It had started in late August 1985, when he and William Griste met with Ochoa in a room at the Miami Airport Hilton Hotel to discuss the cocaine smuggling venture. Ochoa told Wood he'd pay him $1000 per key to get the coke out of Colombia to Abaco Island in the Bahamas and another $2000 per key to portage it into the country. Not long after that Wood and Griste started putting the deal together, meeting with Floyd Sawyer at Marsh Harbour, Abaco Island, to sort things out and to check out some air strips.

Within a month they had flown in 500 keys of coke to Marsh Harbour, Bahamas and, even though they were doing other things with other folks, they had still managed - within a period of 11 months - to transport eight loads. Together, Wood figured, they had imported about 4645 kilograms of cocaine. Wood was the quartermaster, making the payments to the boat pilots, truck drivers, etc. and pocketing what remained of the $8,210,000. Ochoa paid him for the venture. He admitted to having imported literally tons of cocaine and marijuana.

In this business money soon becomes a metaphor for the drugs. One develops a "money problem." You seek it for the mere pleasure of having it. You can't get enough of it. And when you do, you must hide it lest you have to explain it or share it. Or, worse yet, others will know you have it and try to take it away from you. The money becomes just another monkey on your back. Wood, who had been doing this successfully for a few years, had so much green that he had it stacked in five foot high pallets and had the enviable problem of having to figure out what to do with it. His problems became exotic, like, "how much does $1 million weigh?" It was not an unimportant issue. One million in twenties weighs more than one million in hundreds and knowing the weight of any cargo is a necessary fuel consumption calculation. Wood was banking in the Cayman Islands. He told the agents about the plethora of services offered by these "friendly" off shore bankers like "shelf companies," prefab corporations that have already been chartered and which for a fee gets you instantly incorporated there.

He told them about the evolution of their counter-surveillance techniques, beginning with Bobby Eyster. "Bobby asked me if I would pay an additional fee for Christian because he thought we could learn a lot about counter-surveillance and I agreed. Christian brought his equipment and when I saw what he had - he had a spectrum analyzer and a lot more varied UHF antennas and radios than we had previously been using - we started using the same stuff." They had a house trailer at the camp and from there Christian monitored law enforcement transmissions, maintained contact with the plane and communicated with the ground crew.

"A spectrum analyzer can fingerprint or intercept and read any transmitted radio signal. You set it up for certain frequency bands and it will pick up and identify the exact frequency. You can also listen to what is being transmitted on that frequency. It will pick up any frequencies that law enforcement may have used that we weren't already familiar with. In fact, we picked up quite a few more once we start using the spectrum analyzer." It would be nearly another year before Clark's cowboy stunt would finally bring Dickie and his gang down. The breadth of Wood's criminality not only stunned the agents, it sent them in a million directions.

Chapter 11
Local Boy

Sitting on his front porch in Coatapa, Alabama, coffee mug in hand, Tony Chambless watched as a car drove up the dirt road to his modest farm home. United States Customs Service Special Agent Thomas Corum had driven down from Birmingham and was looking into a 512 kilogram cocaine importation in sleepy little Sumpter County, the ass-end of the Northern District of Alabama. Wood had identified a "Tony" - White male, mid-30s, 5 feet 10 inches tall, 180 pounds, with dark hair and a beard, who worked for a paper company in the Demopolis area - as the camp contact. Corum had asked around Livingston. Had left his card at the local Board of Health where a friend of Tony's just happened to work and here came Coram asking questions. Scared out of his mind, Tony knew what he had to do.

He expurgated his guilt. He spilled his guts. He sat down and told the agent everything about the hunting camps, one of them near him in Sumter County. These guys, he told him, used the camps as home bases for operations that would fly loads of cocaine into nearby strips. They had fancy radio equipment and power generators and flood lights that they used to construct an impromptu landing strip. They would synchronize the arrival of the airplanes, the offload crews and the courier vehicles. The contraband would land, be taken away and the field dismantled, all in the wink of an eye. He spewed it out in a tumble. Dickie and Ricou, he said, came to visit him with their plan, assuring him that there was nothing to worry about. "I never did say, 'yes', I would. I never did say, 'no', I wouldn't. You know, I didn't really answer either way. And Dickie told me that if I would just go down there and stand at the gate they would give me $25,000. Just to stand at the gate. And I told him that I still didn't know if I wanted to do it or not. That's when Dickie said 'Well, what you want to do, work the rest of your life?'"

Coram pressed for further details. "Dickie called me on the telephone and told me, he said, 'What we discussed the other night, we are fixing to do it. We need you to get us a step ladder and a big funnel and we'll be up there, you know, in a day or two.' He didn't give no specific date. I carried it up to the camp and left it out there. Next day I run into Steve at Sparky's Grocery down there, which is right near my house, and he told me that they was here, you know, he said 'come on over.'"

Chambless acknowledged that he had previously shown them the airstrip. "We went straight down to the airstrip in the swamp. Dickie gave me a radio. He just told me to keep it and, you know, if I seen anybody headed into the gate, just to, you know, to get on the radio and tell him. I was down there about three hours. The radio was making static and I got scared and turned it off." He went on, blathering to the agent that in his fright he had backed away from the gate, laid on the ground and covered himself in leaves. "I heard the plane. There was a house about 150 to 200 yards at the same end of the strip. By the time he got over the top of the house he turned on his landing lights and really looked like it just lit up everything and then he was right over the top of me in no time. He just came right over the end of the strip where I was and he started going down. A few minutes went by and I heard the plane take off again."

Dickie, Chambless said, came back to offer him a ride. Tony was visibly shivering and joked with Dickie. "I don't know if I'm shaking from the cold or if it's because I'm scared to death" and they all laughed. "Well," Dickie said, " down in the jungle where Ricou is, it's probably 90 degrees, ain't that right Woody?" Corum interrupted; "Who is Woody?" "He's the other pilot." They now had a local corroborating what Wood had told them and connecting Wood to Lynn.

Chapter 12
Ground Control

On the day of his initial arrest in St. Petersburg, Wood had been accompanied by David Carlson, one of his pilots. Carlson had orchestrated a side deal on the sale of the plane either on the sly or in cahoots with Wood. The seller gave Carlson a cool $30,000 cash commission. Carlson may or may not have failed to report that cash. But, he certainly lied to the Customs agents who interviewed him and that is a felony. They had asked him questions but already knew most of the answers. They knew he had contacted the aircraft broker with the sales tip for the Cessna Citation. Not only had Carlson put the two together, it was Carlson and Wood who had inspected the plane. When the broker found the plane "Bishop" wanted, it was Carlson and Wood who were at the meeting. It was Carlson who used the Bishop identity for Wood. He even extended the facade to an introduction of Wood's wife as Carol Bishop. Wood agreed to put a $200,000 deposit on the aircraft, paying the amount in cash. On the day they closed the deal, Carlson and Wood paid the final $885,000 payment by presenting the salesman with three duffel bags of cash. Carlson would also soon be implicated in Carol Wood's bribery fiasco. And, of course, there was his good old buddy Woody, who gave him up.

Carlson rolled. In his debriefing he told Customs Agent Donald Schmidt that he flew a "Chris" from Florida to Alabama, identifying him as a former commercial airline pilot and a counter-surveillance specialist. Chris loaded, he told them, a large piece of equipment onto the plane, something called a spectrum analyzer and used it to monitor law enforcement frequencies. Carlson's statement sent them back to Wood who would eventually identify Christian Schmidgall as the communications man. Schmidgall's specialty was "running radios" (monitoring law-enforcement frequencies and maintaining contact with the pilots). The agents who went to see Schmidgall couldn't help but notice the 52 and 43-foot radio antenna towers at his Lighthouse Point residence. They wanted to ask him questions, they told him, but he sent them packing. A week later he decided to cooperate. He was debriefed on January 26, 1988 in the office of William Shockley, Assistant United States Attorney for the Southern District of Florida.

Schmidgall, who had started out the year cooperating with the authorities in South Florida, would end the year in a wholly different posture. On December 5, 1988 he traveled to Birmingham to meet with Assistant United States Attorney Joe McLean. Schmidgall gave an extensive debriefing, giving the Alabama investigators a comprehensive overview. He began with his first involvement with marijuana importations into the Keys and culminated with the 521 kilogram load into Demopolis on December 16, 1985. His connection, he told them, was Bobby Eyster and William Wood. It was Schmidgall's counter surveillance that had averted their capture during a previous smuggling operation. Some months later, Schmidgall was conscripted for another trip and this time they successfully dropped 35 bales of marijuana into the ocean for which Schmidgall was paid $5,000. Wood introduced Schmidgall to Fabio Ochoa and his partner Bill Griste. He told the investigators that after meeting Ochoa he was asked to deliver radio equipment to another smuggler in the Bahamas and, so, was now a permanent member of this clique.

Schmidgall gave them a complete account of the ill-fated Bahamas cocaine importation. He was hired by Eyster, he told the agents, to monitor the radios. Bill Griste, who was responsible for the boat crew, got arrested in the Bahamas and the rest of the crew panicked and left. Schmidgall orchestrated communications between the pilots, Wood, and a second retrieval team. But the nightmare did not end, Schmidgall told the interviewers. The boat, containing 500 kilograms of cocaine, broke down yet again and Wood personally piloted the repaired boat back to Marathon.

His Alabama involvement began during the December, 1985 load into Sumter County to a hunting camp owned by Lynn and Deshaw. David Carlson flew his equipment to the hunting camp, he told them, giving them full details of the equipment installation, the layout of the camp, the logistics of the entire operation, and the identities of the participants, one of whom turned out to be Chambless. The debriefing was adjourned and scheduled to continue the following day. The agents' notes reflect that there had been some sort of conflict between Schmidgall and his handlers. He was appalled to hear McLean clarify for him that "No, you are not a secret agent, you are a target." Schmidgall, now "half-pregnant," did not return the following day. Instead, what followed was a series of nasty letters between his lawyer and the Assistant United States Attorneys in Florida and Alabama. Because he had given a debriefing in the Southern District of Florida in January and a debriefing in Birmingham in December, his lawyer filed what are called *Kastigar* motions seeking to enforce a deal. The case would have to proceed without Schmidgall as either a witness or as a co-defendant, but that did not keep the government from using the information he provided. Or, from indicting him in the Northern District of Alabama.

Back in Mobile, Odom read Chambless' and Schmidgall's debriefings and had a pretty good idea about where to look. He started sniffing around the Perry County airstrips. On the day of the Schmidgall debriefing, he had gone to Vaiden Field, standing on the very spot where Bob Clark would make his daring escape just two days later. The noose was tightening.

Chapter 13
Cowboy Bob

Odom's decision to "catch and release" the small fish paid off handsomely. Within a month, the two pilots and their attorney were sitting in the Birmingham United States Attorney's office being interviewed by Assistant United States Attorney Joe McLean and the agents. A "debriefing" is an interview that is part of what's called in fed speak a "proffer." It's *Let's Make a Deal.* Usually a defendant in a federal prosecution is in an uneven bargaining position. The government makes all the rules and they make them to favor the prosecution. Someone like Pruna or Wood - those who have a lot of information - do relatively well. But the little fish have no one to hand over. Except when they're the first ones to the courthouse and what they have to offer are the big fish. The two pilots were here to make a deal and were ready to give them the background and the structure of what by now the feds were calling the Dickie Lynn Organization. The first cut by Clark and Abbott was the deepest. They got total immunity. They would not be prosecuted if they cooperated fully with the government.

Odom wanted it all, beginning with the Vaiden Field escapade. "We were refueling when the cops showed up and all hell broke loose. I decided to leave," Clark told him. "I knew that I had landed one way to the northwest, that I could turn around and make it the other way. So I hit the lights. They had lights on and they headed for me and I headed for them and then we kind of headed away from each other as I broke ground. I had enough time to, after I became airborne, to roll slightly to the right to bring the left wing up so the cops couldn't see the numbers on the aircraft."

Clark dismissed the idea that he could have gotten himself or the officers killed. "I've been in closer situations than that, unintentionally. There was wing tip clearance and he was on one side, one-half of the runway and I was on the opposite half of the runway." "What was your escape plan?" McLean asked. "Our escape plan was to not get caught," he shot back.

"Since we hadn't finished refueling, the airplane was loaded heavily on the left side. We were panicked and trying to decide where we were going to go next. We'd been told to go to Huntsville. But we were supposed to have gotten a number that we never got. We didn't have our navigational maps. Muscle Shoals was the only place that we could spot on our little airport directory that might be able to handle us. We landed and parked away from a lighted FAA building. The rest you know."

The plane held 600 kilograms of cocaine, Clark told him. "From Belize?" Odom asked. "No. We changed that route. We went over by Swan Island and then due west to a point where we would stay clear of Cuba and then we cut northwest near Cancun and Cozumel and picked up the 88." The "88," he explained, is the line of longitude that runs through Mobile Bay. "Fred told me that he had flown in at 3,500 feet, sometimes 1,500 feet, but if I stayed at 1,200 to 1,500 feet, things would be fine. I flew it at 800 feet, just to be safe."

Clark had been a commercial pilot, got busted and met Dickie at the federal prison in Eglin. After he got out, Dickie called him one day and they set up a meeting in New Orleans. That's when he met the other pilot, Fred Hartley. They discussed the "flight envelope" and satisfying himself that everything was kosher as far as communications, flight procedures, and so forth, he came on board. The plane would be electronically "swept" to ensure that there hadn't been any bugs placed on board. The group had a high frequency communications system with three stations, one north of Ft. Lauderdale, one in the Keys and one in Alabama. They had a list of twelve frequencies and communicated with the pilot on his return every hour.

They would leave from Tamiami in South Florida, cruise at about 3500 feet, 135 degrees, down to Grand Inagua, turn slightly to 155 degrees, hit Haiti, at which point they would turn to 180 degrees and hit the peninsula, probably 55 or 60 miles from Port-au-Prince. With navigational instruments not really usable they would turn to 192 degrees until they picked up the beacon at Santa Marta, Colombia and from there to some strip off of the coast.

On the return, they would cruise to a point north of San Andres Island, staying below the radar that might pick them up and headed North. Using their DMA (distance measuring device) to tell them how far and in what direction they were from San Andres, they would fly within 30 or 40 miles of the coast of Nicaragua, pick up the beacon at Swan Island and then into Belize. "About 20 minutes out we'd inform 'Short Stop' which is Belize that we were coming in. We'd land, refuel, and take off headed home." They would be paid $140,000 for the trip and had made about $1.1 million.

Chapter 14
Show Time

On June 1, 1989, the prosecution of the 18-count indictment charging Lynn, Deshaw and twenty-one other defendants with numerous drug crimes began in Mobile, Alabama. The indictment had issued months earlier but had been "sealed" because the government had infiltrated the group and was working undercover. The indictment named Lynn in fourteen of the counts, the most serious of those a Continuing Criminal Enterprise charge. Lynn and Deshaw were both accused of being "Drug Kingpins" under a statute that carried a mandatory life sentence. Lynn was said to be the principal administrator and Deshaw his aide-de-camp. They were alleged to have used a sophisticated communications system administered by Bobby Eyster. It was charged that the group would arrive at various hunting camps, communicate with other members of the group who were simultaneously arriving from throughout the United States as well as with the pilots en route from Columbia. This, the government maintained, had resulted in the delivery of almost 16 tons of cocaine into Alabama.

The undercover investigation was stopped supposedly because the agents began to hear some worrisome things. They had at least two somewhat credible- sounding threats made during the undercover tapes and wanted to avoid the Monday morning quarterbacks that would follow some unforeseen disaster. To avoid even the possibility of looking like they had actually assisted a disaster, the agents decided to shut the gang down. On May 6, 1989, the government started arresting the group. Odom was faced with the problem of finding Lynn, effecting his arrest in the safest manner possible and getting a search warrant for his home in order to look for corroborating evidence such as documents, money, and, maybe, even drugs. They didn't know where Lynn lived. Lynn used aliases and did not really maintain a static residence. Abbott and Clark told him that Lynn's house was in Sarasota but couldn't offer much more.

The agents traced Lynn's wife's car and found it parked at the Tampa International Airport. Lynn was driving it! And he was there to pick up Purvis. The two of them returned to a residence on Ocean Boulevard in Sarasota. They now had the location of Lynn's home and had a bead on Purvis as well. The agents spent the following week following Lynn and establishing the surveillance that would help corroborate the recordings made during the undercover meetings. In the end, Odom arrested Dickie quite simply. He had Clark call Lynn to meet him at the airport and when he did, they arrested him. The search of the home, his condo, and personal vehicles yielded a treasure trove of documents such as his income tax reports and mortgages and numerous luxury items such as jewelry and cars. On September 11, 1989, a mere three months after the opening of the case, only five defendants remained, Lynn, Deshaw, Marshall, Eyster, and Craig Keaser. United States District Judge Charles "Randy" Butler would try the case in Mobile, home base of the 13-county United States District Court for the Southern District of Alabama.

The "Port City" is guarded on its eastern frontier by a river. One is delivered physically and temporally under this Stygian barrier by the Bankhead Tunnel and onto Government Street, a stately thoroughfare that sweeps you into an almost too-cliched vision of times past: a dense burrow of magnificent oaks bedecked with veils of Spanish moss that frame manicured lawns of gracious Antebellum and opulent post-modern homes. If you interstate-traveled here, you suffered hundreds of miles of nothing more than the trough of pine trees and concrete and shopping center ubiquity. You may have thought the arid state of Florida to be tropical. But in Mobile, where the country really begins to be lush, you know you are at last truly in the Deep South. You have crossed the confluence of rivers that is the Mobile Delta and now have entered a cultural hyperbaric decompression chamber; This tunnel that was built as part of the "make work" New Deal and bears the name of a famous actress' political ancestor, his pedigree established only by her fame, this city, and even the street's name, which eventually capitulates to urban sprawl and modernism by renaming itself a Boulevard once it forays past the interstate, are all metaphors for the devolvement of the region.

And its gothic politics. Before the Sixties, the South had been morbidly Democratic. Republicans in Alabama met like secret sleeper cells of the Communist Party and the too- few White Republicans that existed were generally centered around the industrial capital of its two largest cities. That would soon change and while the catalyst was mostly social, it was also economic. Birmingham, once an industrial contender because of its steel production, had been bypassed. And no wonder. Its main industry was completely in decline. It was bounded on the north by Memphis and Nashville and on its eastern border by its superstar sister city Atlanta. Mobile fared not much better. In the competition with nearby New Orleans, Mobile was no more than an ugly stepsister. Where once the region had been privy to much of the Democratic Party largesse, this too soon evaporated because of the region's petulant resistance to change. The GOP ran itself off of a cliff in 1964 by nominating Barry Goldwater for President. Lyndon Johnson would punish Mobile by closing Brookley Air Force Base, one of the service's Air Materiel Areas. The closure of the base was a severe economic blow to the city. It dove-tailed with the emerging Civil Rights crisis. The immediate positive result for Alabama's Lost Cause Republicans was that it established an important Southern beachhead by putting five of their kind into the House of Representatives and one of those places was Mobile.

Mobile has always had an air of tolerance to it. It shares more of the history and character of New Orleans than with any other part of the state of Alabama. Like the Big Easy, it has a well-established port, so the city is tied more to the maritime industry than agriculture, the mainstay of the rest of the state. While much of Upper Alabama sports a rugged and scraggy topography, Mobile is part of the Gulf of Mexico's narrow band of tropical flatlands. There are no mountains here, but there are distinctive beaches and expansive horizons. Along with the other cities of the Gulf corridor - Pensacola, Biloxi, Pass Christian, New Orleans - it is defined by the history of the Spanish and French invasions and actively shares these cultural links with these other cities. For example, Mobile and New Orleans spar for bragging rights over just who the hell it was started this thing called Mardi Gras. After World War II, Mobile rocketed from a sleepy, small town to a city with dreams of becoming a true metropolis. Brookley Air Force base broadened the city's cultural base and often these officers, contractors and airmen found the charm of the Port City so alluring that they stayed here. And that influx had been just the latest in a long series of in-migrations. The city - and this included its political establishment - has always boasted a wider range of ethnic groups than its upstate neighbors. Washed ashore by the maritime industry or recruited by land speculators, Greeks, Lebanese, French, Germans and all sorts of others moved here. It is also a Catholic enclave in a state that long considered Papism, like the Party of Lincoln, to be an abomination and has only recently made an unsteady peace with it. And so, here they were, these new GOP stalwarts - they had a tendency to be homegrown, younger, better-educated, and true progressives - converted to what they saw as a reform movement, toiling in the vineyards against the indolence and corruption of the Democratic Party.

And there was plenty to till. The Democratic Party in the South operated like a confederation of political machines headed by plantation-style bosses. These fiefdoms controlled everything and, because they did, often they were the purveyors of the corruption that was so prevalent here. One Alabama governor is purported to have settled a paternity suit with the proceeds of money bilked out of the state's alcohol control board. Asked about his administration's corruption, he's reported to have unabashedly bragged about his own version of the trickle down theory; he would get his but leave enough for others. But now, the country was internally conflicted and nowhere more so than in the South. The party and the region became the prism though which the country sought to examine itself. That was the beginning of the rise of the GOP. One of the vanguard Goldwater Five was Jack Edwards of Mobile. His election energized the Republicans and established the Port City as an important state and national geopolitical foothold.

By 1971, Charles "Randy" Butler, five years out of the University of Alabama Law School and riding the GOP wave of reform, became District Attorney. Although, strictly speaking a Yankee, Butler is as close to the local epithet of "being born under an azalea bush" as any Mobilian can get, even to his 36608 accent, the mellifluous and utterly discernable dialect spoken by the well-connected of that silk stocking zip code. He had been a prosecutor, public defender, and member of one of the city's king-maker law firms. That got him President Reagan's nomination for United States District Judge. Ultraconservative, he had the other criteria Reagan sought, someone young and bright, someone who would outlive the old man and would keep the dream alive.

A trial involving 16 tons of cocaine might be nothing more than the toll of a crazy South Beach weekend, but in Alabama, it is HBO and the director of this drama was none other than the United States Attorney for the Southern District of Alabama himself. Jefferson Beauregard Sessions, like Butler, had been instrumental in upending the political tables in Alabama. A slight man with small town ideals, Sessions is a product of the rural part of the 13-county district he served, having been born and raised in nearby Monroe County. He attended a small local college where he was active in the Young Republicans and, after obtaining the requisite University of Alabama Law School degree, he landed a job as a federal prosecutor in Mobile in 1975.

By 1981 his political chops had jelled. Ronald Reagan nominated him for the chief slot and, not more than five years later, he would nominate him for a vacant federal judgeship. Sessions, the law and order superstar vindicator, had taken the helm of this Class A prosecution and had assigned his best assistant, Gloria Bedwell. The Assistant United States Attorney charged with prosecuting drug crimes in the Southern District of Alabama, Bedwell has known only one adult job, what she calls "putting bad guys in jail." A hard-shell Christian, she is also a true believer in what she does and marries the two with a zealot's passion.

It was lost on no one that the defendants, too, had brought their "A" game. The lead defendants were represented by two of Miami's best lawyers and another from Tampa. Representing Lynn was Roy Black. Today, Black is a television fixture, having gained celebrity lawyer status through his defense of the high profile William Kennedy Smith, Kelsey Grammar, and Rush Limbaugh cases. But even back then, he had more than a few notches on his belt, having gained notoriety for the infamous "Miami cop" and the Sal Maglutta cases. Gentility is much prized here and Black's "style" - he's been called avuncular - fit in nicely with the patrician grace of Mobile and the court. Black was self-effacing and totally unflashy. His appearance did nothing to dispel the professorial aura about him. Tall, gawky and bookish, he had a baby face and was completely devoid of any apparent arrogance or conceits. He relished doing the mundane, like hanging out in the Spanish-style plaza called Bienville Square and feeding the squirrels peanuts from the local A&M nut store. He seemed absolutely enthralled with the small town delights, like having his shoes fixed at the Dauphine Shoeteria or getting homemade candy from the Three George's Candy Store, a soda shop right out of *Happy Days*. He loved the languid pace, waxing on endlessly about the City's grace and style and everyone's friendly attitude.

While Bronis and Black took turns playing Mutt and Jeff, the "bad cop" role would more naturally and often fall to Bronis. But Black is no pushover. This is a guy that helped lionize the Miami Public Defenders' office and who, even in Miami, carried superstar status. And, it was obvious that all talents that are forged in the crucible of that office are stellar. Black, who spent five years as one of the lead defenders and then as a criminal evidence instructor at the University of Miami, had complete mastery of the case and of criminal law and criminal procedure. Where a local criminal defense lawyer might ask for his "Jencks" discovery, Black would ask for his "18 United States Code Section 3500 material."

Bennie Lazzara of Tampa represented Ricou Deshaw. Lazzara had gained a reputation first as a prosecutor then as a defense lawyer, most notably, the "Pizza Hut Murders." Like Black, he was tall and lanky and, also like Black, his style was laid back and almost self-effacing. Although he represented the second lead defendant, Lazzara mostly kept out of the way. It would turn out to be a wise tactic. Bobby Eyster was represented by Miami's Stephen Bronis. Bronis had also cut his teeth with the Public Defender. But, he and Black were Yin and Yang. Eyster, accused of being one of the communications persons in the conspiracy, was actually a secondary character but you would not know that if you judged it by the heat of his defense. A small man of dark complexion, Bronis was aggression incarnate, a Charles Bronson to Black's Alan Alda who exuded raw charisma. He was devastating. He had the inside knowledge of so many drug world machinations and a complete mastery of trial tactics and techniques. His cross-examination of the government's chief witnesses was masterful and blistering.

A trial is an orchestrated series of images one-dimensionally flattened by the rules of evidence and trial procedure and the necessity to present the oh-too-many mundane facts that require proof. Another limitation and one of the major differences between a federal and a state trial is the scope given to the questions made by lawyers. Even in Alabama, state trial procedure is much more open to the rough-and-tumble of cross-examination and trial tactics that is your typical movie fare. A prosecutor's job is to try and make them come across like a Busby Berkeley spectacular, usually through "sexy" witnesses, like Wood and Pruna. While she might seem outmatched by the likes of this flashy big city talent, Bedwell is a remarkably intelligent woman, a Phi Beta Kappa and Magna Cum Laude graduate and an accomplished trial lawyer. As the lead attorney for the Organized Crime Drug Enforcement Task Force (OCDETF) for the Southern District of Alabama, she is often called upon to single-handedly prosecute multi-defendant cases. If the big city boys wanted a piece of her, well, they had better pack a lunch. Her style is not flashy. She prefers to concentrate on trial preparation and a plain, linear, and grinding method of presentation. Busby Berkeley? No. Her stories are skillful and precise paint-by-2-number black-and-white documentaries.

It would be Butler's first major trial and he would handle the complicated multi-defendant high-profile Lynn case in such an efficient and professional manner that it would come to typify a signature courtroom style. While Butler has real respect for the law, his philosophical views have a tendency to narrow the windows of his receptors. Intellectually honest enough to see the merit of a real argument, he rewards good lawyering and is not afraid to make an unpopular or impolitic decision. He runs a clean fight but brooks no nonsense. He is the classic iron hand in the velvet glove. Extremely gifted and with strong political and religious views, Butler is intellectually brilliant, honest and agile. Outwardly emotionally flat and measured, there is not one an iota of pyrotechnics to his demeanor. He can be both pragmatic and doctrinaire. He is obsequiously courteous in the manner of the Gothic South, even when wreaking disastrously devastating results and he was no different with his out-of-town guests. He was clearly respectful and almost deferential to them and closely considered their arguments. Butler, who hadn't as yet developed the clinical and restrictive federal view, gave his guests uncharacteristically wide leeway.

Chapter 15
Ground Crew

The great Frank and Ernest quip about Ginger Rogers - that while Astaire was indeed great, that she had to dance backwards and in high heels - is an apt criminal defense metaphor. The defense has to be ready for whatever comes at them and in whatever order the other side proceeds. The prosecution has home court advantage, favorable procedural rules, and, oh yes, those pesky facts. Defense lawyers know how to dip and sway and Bedwell's first substantive lead was Lynn's lifelong friend Stephen Purvis. He supplied both credible biographical information and intriguing details about the minutia of drug trafficking.

Purvis, Ricou and Dickie became friends when he was six or seven years old. They had all played ball together. He had been their quarterback for the Coral Shores Hurricanes and the second baseman for the Tavernier Tigers. They played basketball. They had always been a team. He had worked for Lynn's brother doing construction after high school and he knew Jack Marshall, also from doing construction work together. Purvis and Deweese had become Lynn's lieutenants when the others had fallen out of the picture and then had taken Dickie's place when he quit.

His first involvement in trafficking, Purvis said, was with Dickie Lynn. They had taken a boat around 1981 to the Grand Bahamas Bank and marijuana was airdropped to them and they would bring it back in cigarette boats. "When we went down to the Grand Bahamas Bank, it would be at sundown and the stuff out in the bay, when we switched to cocaine, was done at night with a boat on each end, a half a mile apart, with a light for the airplane to drop in between the two lights."

He recounted the incident in the Keys when the Air Force jet had scrambled to intercept the airplane and, in the process, he put it on Eyster as being the communications man. Radios, he told the jury, were used to maintain communications between the plane and the boats. That scare had been the catalyst for moving the operation to Alabama. "Nobody said anything about the airdrop going awry. I was on the bay the day they scrambled the jet fighters. The one working the radio informed us that they were scrambling the jets. The airplane came over the Keys and the airplane had to go back to wherever it went to. I am not sure where it went."

His first trip was for Dickie and Woody. His role had been to set up the lights and work one of the three generators about two or three hours before the arrival of the airplane. He was paid around $50,000 for helping unload the airplane, refueling it, and picking up the lookouts on the way out. "We strung lights up and put them together with the extension cords at 50-foot intervals and we had three generators to power lights. The airplane came in and I was at a middle generator. So we were told just to stay where we were because it took a matter of just a couple of minutes to unload the airplane and we had two-meter radios and then the plane would land and we would turn the lights out immediately and would turn the lights back on and the product would leave and the plane would leave and after that a couple of guys would stay and roll up the cords and the lights and take everything back to camp." The freezer at the camp had a lock on gear. He was told that the average trip was for 600 kilograms of cocaine but he never counted. "Naturally, you don't count something like that. There were duffel bags, I would estimate 8 or 10 of them."

Because the radios couldn't reach out from Alabama all the way to Belize or South America, radio communications were maintained between the planes and a communications center at the hunting camp. "When we moved up to working in Alabama, Bobby Eyster worked the radios with us." They would monitor the local police station, fire department, Coast Guard, and any radio transmissions. There was a radio unit in the truck so they could talk to the camp on a handheld.

He was involved with two more trips involving the grass airfield.

The lights were a hassle, he said, and there was a tendency for fog off the river and there were trees on either side of the field so they moved to the Demopolis airfield. But this required a lot more reconnaissance. "We did a lot more on the airfield after we started going over there which was just to make sure nobody was coming in and out of it on any kind of time schedule, seeing what time the fog developed and later on we didn't do a lot of that."

Purvis also helped flesh out the details behind the load that had been left in Waynesboro. "We were at the Demopolis field waiting for the airplane to arrive and I remember specifically because the night was very clear, crystal clear, and within a half-hour it was completely fogged in. The airplane advised us they couldn't land, although they tried to, and that they wanted to take it back to New Orleans and then try to come back with it the following night." Dickie told Bagalman to just go back to New Orleans and park the plane on a ramp. Instead, they had abandoned it on the end of a runway in who knows where. They were angry, he told the jury. They had to go look for the load. Dickie slammed the receiver down on the payphone and told the others. "God damn idiots. They left the load in Waynesboro. We have to go and recover it." The big black Suburban and the blue van set out in convoy.

If there's little reason for non-locals to go through Demopolis, there's even less reason to go through Waynesboro, Mississippi. At best, it's a shortcut to Montgomery or New Orleans. But it was close enough to the camp that Dickie figured that saving 700 keys was worth the risk. They scrubbed the mission shortly after arrival. From their observation post at the Waffle House, it was obvious that this sleepy little town was abuzz with all of the activity of a violated ant bed. Cop cars ran amok. Blue lights flashed. Sirens wailed. Lynn, who had been nearby checking it out, radioed the others. "This is Buckwheat, let's book."

But the crash was always center stage and Purvis had been there. He had been "on the ground" along with Dickie, Hillary Deweese and Mike

Barclay. Eyster was at the camp working the radios. "It was pretty standard except right up to just a few minutes before the airplane got there. The south end of the airfield got foggy. Fred Hartley didn't have Marks Bagalman with him. Marks, I had heard, had swindled him out of a large sum of money. So he had his brother Joe flying with him. Fred came in and circled round and on his approach, he crashed. It was a ball of fire in the sky. We drove to the end of the airfield, that is the exit, the only gate or only exit that is not blocked by a gate, and the wreckage was across the exit road and it was on fire. So we turned and went back across the airfield and just drove through a small chain-link fence."

He had also been at Vaiden Field. They got caught because "the pilot radioed that he was very low on fuel and he was having a problem finding the field. So we turned on a large spotlight that we had. We were, naturally, worried about safety. Apparently, there was a guy that worked at the Fixed Base Operation there that called the police and they dispatched some squad cars." The whole thing jumped off in seconds, he said. "When I first saw the blinking lights from the police car, I was just finishing up refueling the wing of the airplane. I was advised by the pilot, he said not to worry about him, that he could get out of there. I jumped in the S-10 pickup and he swung the airplane around and turned off the lights and headed toward the police officers."

"When I looked in the rearview mirrors all I could see was him, naturally, and after he lifted off the ground I could see the blinking blue lights again and eventually they came on down the airstrip after me. I ran the truck off the end of the airstrip." But, he said, it got stuck in the muck and the run was even harder. "About every less than a quarter of a mile you had to stop and peel the mud off your shoes and stuff because otherwise it would keep getting wider and wider until you couldn't walk anymore." Eventually he met up with Barclay and Deweese. "The day before I had done surveillance on the whole area. So I knew the roads and things round there and I proceeded through a couple of ravines and to where some water was. There was an opening on the field and I got on a secondary road and from there I realized if I kept going down the secondary roads that would be the natural place to look for us and we turned around and headed parallel back up the road parallel to the airfield and more or less went right back to the entrance."

"Deweese is fat and a smoker and couldn't keep up with me so I told him to just lay low and I would come back and get him." Purvis got back to the campground around 4:30 in the morning. It had been complicated by the fact that it was hunting season. The hunters start going to their stands. They might run into them, or worse yet, they might be mistaken for another kind of prey and accidentally shot. No keys. They broke into the five-wheel. They had been warned over the radio that the police were looking for a truck with over-the-cab lights. They took some duct tape, covered them up and headed out.

They contacted Deweese and told him they were coming to get him. "It so happened when I pulled out on the highway, I was passed by a squad car with the lights going and everything. I assumed he was pulling me over and when he went on by me and made a left turn at Highway 5 to go back over to the airfield, I radioed Mike and Hillary that I was going to come in behind a police car and pick them up." They headed home.

Chapter 16
The Big Cheese-Eater

A criminal prosecution is a presentation that belies what goes into its making. It's legal sausage, a mishmash of unmentionables not for the squeamish, the mechanics of which are best left unexamined. Justice is a meat factory where process is meted out wholesale on the scales of justice, often by a black-smocked butcher with ten thumbs. Its trickle-down nature is just another chunk of ugly. The more cunning or culpable a person is, the more likely he or she will have something with which to barter. It is not uncommonly described as "the race to the courthouse." It begins with a defendant's opening gambit, an offer ("proffer") to make a deal with the government. After the signing of this agreement which protects the defendant's statement from further prosecution, a "debriefing" follows and the defendant is interviewed. The information is assessed and, if you're good at it and you have something to sell, a deal is cut.

Wood was good at it. By the time of the Lynn trial, he had already testified in the Oklahoma trial of another of their childhood friends. Bedwell's *prima donnas*, Wood and Pruna, had been the target for all of the lawyers' opening remarks. Bronis had characterized Wood as evil incarnate, someone who, until his latest arrest, "had succeeded in using his great skills manipulating and lying to friends and family, to strangers, to the police and to the courts to make a mockery of the criminal justice system," someone who, despite having been caught red-handed in the past, could, with a few equal "chosen lies and promises never meant to be kept," talk himself out of anything. Wood's ascension into the witness box was taut with opening night anticipation.

Drug traffickers tend to gravitate toward specialties, either hauling it or selling it. Lynn and his associates were essentially the transportation franchise but Wood did it all. At the time of William Wood's arrest, a government prosecutor in Florida had happily announced the capture of "the devil and his crew." By trial time, though, like Saul on the road to Damascus, Wood was shining his inner light, describing for the jury his metamorphosis from marijuana offloader to cocaine "salesman" to drug kingpin and, now, a contrite, if somewhat still obviously arrogant, government witness. The feds had taken all sorts of measures to protect Wood, even to the point of booking him under his Stephen Bishop alias at the Hernando County Jail in Florida. Testifying under heavy security measures and by now a twice-convicted federal prisoner who had agreed to forfeit $5 million, he told the jury what he said were his five cocaine deals with these defendants.

Defense lawyers often claim that there is a "drug exception" to the Constitution. That's because many of the prophylactic rules have been constricted and the range of allowable testimony has been expanded, especially in those kinds of cases. The use of hearsay where a drug conspiracy is charged, for example, is allowed under no greater reasoning than that it makes it easier to prosecute what is a "mind crime." A legal issue like whether or not a conspirator is the "hub" or the "spoke" of one or more conspiracies is a subjective call and seems to appear on what is more convenient for the government. It was Wood who was connected to the DTOs (Drug Trafficking Organizations) like the Pruna Brothers, the Cabrera Brothers, Columbians Fabio and Mauricio Ochoa, Gustavo Salazar and a bunch of other folks. His best testimony against Lynn and Deshaw was that he had been involved only five times with them, three and two, respectively. So, while it is no small irony that he was testifying against Lynn and not the other way around, it is par for the course. Wood was serving a 20-year sentence. His other 15-year sentence was concurrent, which meant that it did not add any time to his sentence. He was now avoiding more convictions in Alabama and expected a sentence reduction.

At the sausage factory, not only is the sinner often now the saint, the discussions, like the postulations about the number of angels dancing on the heads of how many pins, are just mental masturbation. No one cares. The juries, even the judges, aren't all that interested in the real intricacies, the niceties and "technicalities" of the law. That's just casing on the sausage. They just want to get to the meat, down to the bone, something Wood was perfectly capable of doing. Wood took the stand and even in his prison garb he was tall and polished and presented quite a commanding figure. He and Ricou had first hooked up he said "March and April of 1983, we did two air drops when we were doing the marijuana air drops off of Marco Island. Back in that time, we first started doing Jamaican marijuana, fly to Jamaica and pick it up. And Ricou wanted to switch to Colombian marijuana and eventually turned to Colombian cocaine. So we flew, I am not exactly sure how many trips, two or three trips of Colombian marijuana and air-dropped them and the same thing, I picked it up and sold it and paid them. I took a commission, percentage for my fee and sold his too and paid him all the money. On the next-to-last trip we did there, he brought back six and a half kilos of cocaine and dropped it in a PVC pipe into the water along with about 1300 pounds of marijuana. I personally brought it ashore. I took it back to Key Largo and eventually turned it over to Mr. Deshaw and they did whatever they wanted to do with it."

"Well, we did one more, except it was strictly cocaine it was done a little differently because I was in jail at the time. We were supposed to do it and I went to jail. I had gotten busted on a marijuana beef down in Charlotte County, Florida. And I had to serve four months in jail. Anyway, we already had arranged to do it but we couldn't pull it off because I had to go to jail. So I left it up to my brother-in-law, a fellow by the name of John Harrison. He was basically doing the work out on the water because I was out on bond and I wasn't taking as much of an active role in bringing it in. I would help sell the marijuana when he came in. Anyway the trip came off. Ricou and Joe had flown in with the cocaine and they dropped it on to John and John had brought her in. I got paid a full share even though I wasn't there."

Wood told the jury that he and Frank Basso had been working for Gustavo Salazar. "Frank came to me and told me that he had a Columbian guy that wanted to bring some cocaine up to the United States and he had secured an airstrip in the Bahamas to use. I went with Mr. Salazar to Rock Sound, that is a settlement in the Bahamas in the Eleuthra Island chain, saw the airstrip and I came back and discussed it with Mr. Deshaw and he agreed to fly the cocaine from Columbia to Rock Sound. And at that time I would boat across from Rock Sound to Key Largo and deliver to Miami. From Rock Sound to Key Largo is approximately 300 miles. We had done this a number of times, between 12 and 15 times with marijuana. So all we did was change the commodities. Otherwise it was basically the same."

"We did two actually," he said. "One in January of '85 and Ricou flew down to Columbia with Kevin Sheehy as the co-pilot." They returned with 18 duffel bags of cocaine, approximately 388 kilos. "Myself and Howard Carrell were waiting on the airstrip when they landed along with a couple of Bahamian natives. We unloaded the cocaine into a truck and took it to one of the native's homes. The boat had broken down on its way over so we stopped and got it fixed." The coke was loaded into the Midnight Express and ferried across where Wood met the load offshore at Tavernier Key and then ran it to shore. "We unloaded the cocaine from the boats. Actually one boat, it was my boat. And myself and Howard Carrell were in that boat. We loaded cars that were owned by Gustavo Salazar and delivered the cocaine to him in Miami. And he, in return, paid me a fee for doing it."

The expenses didn't add up, Wood complained. He had been expecting a larger load. "Everyone was working on set fees in the islands. I was paying off customs and immigration police there. It cost me $300,000 a trip and they didn't care if you only brought in 1 kilogram or 2000." And, too, there are the unforeseen circumstances. The boat had broken down on the first trip, causing added expenses and the loss of their captain. The drama was too much for him and he backed out. That's when

Ricou suggested Lynn. "He said, 'Well, can you use him?' I said, 'Well, to tell you the truth, we need a boat captain.' I told him my other captain had backed out on me."

Ricou and Kevin Sheehy flew to Columbia again, this time bringing back 694 keys of cocaine and 41 duffel bags and flying it to Rock Sound, basically a repeat of the first trip. It was a repeat in more ways than one. Wood and Carrell and two locals unloaded the plane and stored it pending the arrival of the boat. But, again, the boat had broken down. Dickie had made it as far as Bimini but was marooned there for repairs. His first mate had mutinied, saying that "He said he didn't feel good about the trip and he didn't want to go." With Ricou and Kevin already back from Columbia and a monster load of incriminating cocaine already stored in Rock Sound, Wood offered Sheehy $100,000 to act as mate and off he went.

"That time when they came back the weather was horrendous and we met about half a mile offshore of Tavernier Key. We unloaded the cocaine into two boats that time because there were so many bags. We couldn't put it all in one. We loaded one into a boat, my boat, along with Howard Carrell. My brother, Tom, drove the other boat that was loaded. I don't know who rode with him that night. And we ran the cocaine onto the shore and delivered it to Miami." He paid Ricou, he said, $1000 a kilo and Dickie a flat $250,000.

Wood's Columbian connections expanded. "In roughly August of '85," he told the jury, "I ran into an old accomplice of ours, a fellow by the name of Bill Griste and he introduced me to a Colombian individual by the name of Fabio Ochoa in Miami. And they had successfully flown a trip of cocaine into Marsh Harbour in the Abacos in the Bahamas and boated it across." In short order their successful importations supplied Wood with all the cocaine he could sell. And sell it he did. "By that time I turned around and was selling the cocaine by the kilo. I sold massive amounts of cocaine. So they (the Colombians) wanted me to help them, to sell some of their cocaine so they could get their money. They got paid cocaine and that was the method of payment they were given for the work that they had done and they wanted to convert that to dollars so they could pay the crews and take their profits. So I helped them sell it."

Wood's partnership with the Ochoa brothers expanded even further. "One thing led to another and they asked me did I want to send a plane. The plane that they brought up was a Piper Seneca and it had crashed when they landed. It wasn't a severe crash but the landing gear had gotten mangled." Wood told them about some of his experiences in Rock Sound and about his crew. "We were all pretty experienced with each other. So everyone knew they could depend on the other, to depend on what to do. I know Ricou can fly the plane back and Dickie could bring the boat back and they knew I would pay them so that made it a lot easier." Ochoa told Wood to Talk to his folks to see if they were interested,.

It was perfect timing. Ricou and Dickie had just purchased a Navajo Panther Chieftain and they were in the process of customizing it with high frequency radios and fuel tanks that would give them longer range. And, they were most unhappy with the way things were going in Louisiana, Wood told the jury. "They had some kind of a scam where they were going to fly some stuff through Belize and to Louisiana. At that time it fizzled out on them." They had also been warned by a neighbor, a senior customs agent from the Keys that there had been a surveillance report concerning their plane unloading duffel bags in Meridian, Mississippi.

Wood's proposal was that they fly a load of cocaine from Columbia up to Marsh Harbour in the Bahamas. "It was basically the same as we had done before in Rock Sound. It had only been seven or eight months." He would pay them $1000 a kilo on an expected 500-key deal. Half a million bucks? They were in. For the maritime leg of the conspiracy, Wood had purchased a cigarette boat, a 40-foot Performer. Dickie agreed to pilot the boat for $250,000.

Ricou and Fred Hartley flew back from Columbia to a farming area just outside of Marsh Harbour, landed on a dirt road, unloaded 500 keys of cocaine into trucks and, since Bahamian law requires a flight plan for night flights, waited anxiously for daylight to come. The next morning they flew to Nassau, left the aircraft on a ramp and returned by commercial air to Miami.

Woody explained how they had changed the location to Alabama. "I wanted to do the same trip again to Marsh Harbour except we were going to use a Colombian aircraft instead of Ricou and Dickie's. I asked Dickie to drive the boat back and he didn't want to do it. He decided he had enough money. So I came up with another crew and we, in fact, brought 400 kilos of cocaine up from Columbia. When the boat went to come back, it had an accident. It ran aground off of Andros Key and received substantial damage. We managed to salvage the cocaine. And, in fact, I personally went over and got some boats and made some emergency repairs and brought it back to Florida."

His boat damaged and down for a long count, Wood listened to his friends' pitch about Alabama and the hunting camp that they had there. "They had a friend up there, a fellow by the name of Tony, that had shown them the strip while they were up there hunting a month or so earlier and he said, 'Tony showed us a strip out in the back with nothing around it. Why don't we go look at it?'" They rode up there to check it out. "We landed there. They called this fellow Tony and he came over and picked us up in the truck and we drove around to where the strip was. It was around on the other side of the river. It is really only about a mile from the airport depending on the way to get around it because of the river that runs between the two strips. We went around to look at the strip and we measured it with the vehicle to get the distance. We first looked at it from the overhead view. We flew back and forth overhead because it is kind of small. Well, this obviously was something different. We never landed cocaine in this country, actually flown a plane in and landed, none of us had, at least I don't think so. I know I hadn't and I don't believe they had either."

The trio put together a cooperative venture that would use both of their crews. They would fly from Miami to Columbia, pick up the cocaine, refuel in Belize and fly to Alabama. The Belize refueling would be handled by Fred Pou, another New Orleans friend. He would be paid $100,000. Fred Hartley, the pilot, would be paid $300,000. Steve Purvis and David Merrill on the ground in Alabama would be paid $50,000 each. Wood's brother-in-law Howard Carrell would accompany him. Wood insisted on using Christian Schmidgall as his radio person in Alabama and he would also supply the drivers. "At the last moment Fred Poe got busted so we were afraid to use him to go to Belize. So we needed another pilot and we needed someone to handle the ground -- the fuel -- the refueling in Belize. So Ricou suggested he go to Belize and handle the refueling. And they told us they had another pilot they could use. All I know his name was Mark and he's an attorney from the New Orleans area. They wanted to use him. I had never met him but I didn't like the idea of an attorney in the plane flying cocaine. In lieu of that, I flew in the plane. I said, 'Well, I will fly it myself.' So that is how we switched around. I flew with Fred. Ricou was going to handle the ground refueling in Belize and Dickie would run the ground operation in Alabama."

The first gig ran late on the Columbian side. Although some of the merchandise was there, it wasn't even half. "They called us and told us that they had problems on the strip. They made us believe it was some kind of a problem with the police forces or whatever. So we pulled the power back and slowed down. The whole time I was communicating back to the United States by radio. We eventually landed at the strip in Monteria at about 2:30 in the afternoon or something like that. We got there and the cocaine wasn't there or at least a majority of the load wasn't there. There were a number of Colombians there waiting for us. We turned the plane around and refueled, checked the oil and basically sat around for about an hour and a half." Finally, a Cessna 303 came into view. It bore down on the strip, landed from the opposite direction, spun around and quickly threw 400 keys of coke out on the ground. They loaded it and the 120 keys that had arrived by truck, fired up and left for Belize.

The extra waiting had put them way behind schedule. Wood assured Deshaw that everything was okay, but got some assurances of his own. Weather conditions were okay. No police problems. He checked back in with Ricou who was waiting for them in Belize and he, in turn, told "Home Plate." Christian Schmidgall, positioned on a farm outside of Demopolis, was the communications hub. "We were running behind schedule, about two hours. We were anticipating being in Belize around 7:00 or 7:30 and we got in around 9:00. We communicated by two-meter hand-held radios. We landed on a road in Orange Walk in Belize. It was right by a sugar mill. He said 'When I hear you coming I will light it up.' So the next thing you know he says 'Okay I hear you. You are south of me look north.' So we looked off to our right and saw a series of signal flares being lit along each side of the road. So we swung the plane around to the north and landed to the south. We landed the plane and turned it around and we immediately began refueling the aircraft. There was a bunch of Belize natives. They ran out and started refueling the tanks on the plane. I had a bag with $50,000 in cash to pay the person there on the strip. He gave me a bag of chicken to eat on the way back."

They flew up over the Mexican peninsula into the Gulf of Mexico. About 125 miles from Louisiana, they doused their lights and dropped their altitude to about 800 feet, slowing down to 120 kilometers so that the radar would confuse their profile with the helicopters that fly out to and from the oil rigs. Entering the United States just west of New Orleans, they regained altitude, crossed north of New Orleans and flew to Demopolis. "We were communicating the entire time by radio by HF radio, which is High Frequency Radio, which works long-range. When we were on the way to Belize, Christian finally came on the radio and he was positioned in Alabama on the farm up there outside of Demopolis. We gave him a location report of where we were and let him know everything was all right." About 35 miles outside of the Alabama landing strip, Wood checked in with Lynn on the two-meter band. As soon as they heard the plane, the ground crew fired up the generators and lit the floodlights that they had placed around this field. "I called and spoke to Dickie on the ground. We were concerned about fog and about being followed. We made sure Chris had his counter-surveillance on and he told us we were coming clean. When we got to the strip area, there is a paper mill south of the airstrip. We flew around the south side of the paper mill and flew in and we were going to land from the east to the west and we flew in the first time we came in we missed the strip and didn't see it."

"We landed the plane. We were a little concerned because the strip is kind of short but we wound up getting down pretty quick and stopped." The plane's load was taken to the camp where drivers would arrive soon to take loads either back to Miami or up to Detroit. Fred flew the aircraft away from the scene of the crime, back to New Orleans. "As soon as we closed it up, Dickie and I jumped in the cab of the truck. Dickie drove and I rode shotgun and we left immediately." "Did you literally have a shotgun in the truck?" Bedwell asked. "No, I was riding in the passenger's side of the truck. We had an Uzi machine gun."

The ground crew returned to the field to collect the generators and floodlights. Another aircraft, flown up to Demopolis the night before, carried the rest of them and the communications equipment back to Miami where Woody would wait for the arrival of the load cars. The contraband was delivered to the Ochoas and - at a transportation cost of $4000 per kilo - Woody received a $2 million plus payoff.

But that was before expenses. Woody "just took up the scrap," after all the bills were paid. "We had never done a trip like this. And asked them what they wanted for the use of their plane and arranging the landing and the strip and Alabama. They knew about the strip, I didn't, and the Belize refuel and that stuff, and Dickie blurted out 'We want $1 million' and I said 'okay'. But we were anticipating bringing back 600 kilograms of cocaine. When we wound up 79 kilograms short, that caused me a shortfall of money. When I came back, I said 'We didn't get all the load we were supposed to bring. Can you guys accept $800,000? And they both said 'Yes.'"

Elated at the success of their venture, Woody and Dickie flew up to Demopolis a week later. "It was sometime in January, I got a phone call from Dickie. He told my wife to tell me to meet him at the Demopolis Airport," Tony Chambless would testify. "I thought he was probably coming up to hunt. I sat there a little while and then Dickie and Woody landed. Dickie said 'I brought you a Christmas present' and handed me a rifle. We all walked to my truck to put it away and Woody gives me this wad of money. It was $50,000. I said that I hadn't done nothing to get that money and Dickie said 'You did what we wanted you to do.'" It was supposed to be only $25,000, Tony reminded them. Woody said that "Everything went real well and we are going to give you 50." They continued on to New Orleans where, also as a reward for a job well done, Dickie presented Hartley with some alligator skin boots. Woody gave him a $7,000 18-karat Rolex watch and, of course, his $300,000 cut.

Chapter 17
The Consigliere

Marks Bagalman effortlessly matched every negative stereotype one can have about lawyers and it was his rascality that probably saved his life. Accused by Lynn of ripping them off, he had been cut out and replaced by Fred Hartley's brother Joe. It would be Joe's first and only trip. Odom, who had been following leads as far back as the Meridian drop, doubled down on his efforts because of the crash. He connected Bagalman through the purchase records found inside the wreckage. Some lucky leads and good detective police work led him to a girlfriend, to dental records and a positive identification of the Hartleys as the pilots. He started poking about in Louisiana and began by looking into Bagalman.

The defense had great sport with him. He was a shifty and evasive opportunist who carried plenty of slimy baggage, even showing up for rehab with ounces of cocaine in his luggage. He had been involved in plenty of shady deals. He was, as they say in Alabama, as "sorry as white dog shit." Bronis would begin his characteristically blistering cross-examination by reading the oath that lawyers take upon admission to the bar. He admitted that he knew about and assisted his best friend Hartley in making investments, none of which he had bothered to turn over to estate heirs for distribution. He had even managed to extort $50,000 from Lynn as hush money. His testimony was shot through with inconsistencies and vagueness and while he portrayed himself as just a hapless addict, it was clear that he had been a major player. Comic relief notwithstanding, Bagalman provided details and corroboration about the flights from Columbia into Alabama. He was the only one still alive that could give the details about the abandoned load at Waynesboro.

Bagalman admitted to making 1 to 1.2 million dollars for his participation in drug smuggling. He had gotten introduced to Lynn through

Gary Young, for whom he testified he was "doing legal work." A few weeks later they met at Bart's, Young's restaurant in New Orleans to discuss smuggling marijuana. "We discussed whether my friend at the time Fred Hartley would in fact fly one airplane. It was my understanding that Dick and Rick would fly another airplane." They went to Lakefront Airport, where they tried a dry run. "On board was myself, Dick, Rick, and Fred. We had, like, a little cooler, ice chest, Styrofoam ice chest. This was the first time I had ever seen a Loran in an airplane. Evidently somebody had found a place west of Baton Rouge where this alleged marijuana air drop was going to take place because he had the coordinates in his Loran." Deshaw showed Bagalman how to eject the marijuana bales.

During mid-July of 1985, they made the first of several trips. The plan called for two planes flying in tandem. Lynn and Deshaw would fly the Cessna 404 Titan, and Marks and Fred would fly Bagalman's plane. They landed in Belize, refueled, and took off with 1,500 pounds of marijuana in each plane and headed back to Louisiana. Somehow they lost track of the Titan but they pushed on. "We went to the same spot that Ricou had taken us on that trip where he was showing us his airplane. I believe the name of the place is Butte LaRose just west of Baton Rouge, Louisiana. It is a series of canals in some marsh land, and that was the predetermined spot to do an airdrop of marijuana. I recall seeing a light in the canal. And I believe we had a radio on board the airplane and made contact with somebody on the ground. And when we determined that it was, in fact, the right spot, we made three passes down a straight portion of the canal. On each pass, I would be in the back of the airplane pushing out the bales of marijuana. Prior to that I would put these little green light sticks on them so they could be seen by the ground crew."

Two days later, Lynn and Deshaw came to Bagalman's house. They had lost the second half of the load. "He was trying to leave this make-do airstrip in Belize, it was kind of muddy, he had a very heavy airplane, wide airplane, large wing span, it slid off the road or runway and ran into the trees. They unloaded the marijuana and burned the airplane." They wanted Bagalman to go back with Hartley to get the load but he refused so Hartley and Deshaw returned to Belize in Bagalman's plane and got the rest of the load.

They had lost a plane and the other one was connected to it. It was time for new planes. Bagalman titled the Lynn/Deshaw plane to one of his companies. In return, they agreed to pay him a $20,000 per trip commission. They met him at a South Florida dealership and handed him a suitcase full of cash to cover the purchase. They gave Bagalman a suitcase containing enough cash to cover a check for the plane, which he later claimed had been short.

Around Christmas 1985, Bagalman ran into Lynn and Wood at the New Orleans Airport. They were on their way to see Hartley, which made Bagalman suspicious. He figured that they were going to cheat him out of a load commission and confronted Hartley who admitted that he had already flown a load. "He told me that he flew to Columbia. I remember he told me he to flew to Columbia with William Wood. And they came back, landed in Belize for refueling with a gentleman named Freddy Pou and from there went to a place right next to Demopolis, Alabama, some grass strip. He said, 'You got to see this place. It is lit up at night better than Moisant International.'" Bagalman was infuriated. He wanted his usage fee. Hartley had gotten $200,000 for the first trip, and $300,000 for the second one. Hartley mollified him by promising him half of his fee as co-pilot on the next cocaine load.

Bagalman was now on board and for his first cocaine trip, he flew to Miami to meet Hartley, Lynn and Deshaw. Hartley had just returned from a third trip but within a few days, they were plotting a new one. Deshaw and Lynn came by the hotel to go over some maps and lay out a basic route and the times that they were to check in using High Frequency Radio (HF) to check in. "We were given a series of channels in case we couldn't reach anybody on a particular channel. We were to wait five minutes and go to the next one, wait five minutes and go to the next one. Just keep attempting to call." It was from Fred's fetish for the Peanuts character Snoopy, he testified, that they had gotten their code names. "He had a tattoo on his arm of that particular character. He was referred to as 'Snoopy' and there were several radio points, one allegedly located in Miami, that was referred to as 'Baron' or 'Red Baron'. There was the place in Demopolis which was referred to as 'Home Plate.' And Belize, the refueling point, was referred to as 'Shortstop.'"

They initially departed from Tamiami Airport, would fly to Colombia and return to Alabama with Belize as the refueling point. "This particular trip we laid out a route to get to Columbia which took us directly, when I say directly, midway of Cuba. And we didn't have anybody on board. Just Fred and I. We were given basic coordinates for the Loran to lead us to a particular destination in Columbia. We had an approximate place circled on a section of map. But the further south we got, the more unreliable the Loran became. And it would click in and click out and we didn't know if it was reading correctly or not. So we tried to use some visual sightings according to the map. And we were having difficulty. We were told that we would know the strip because they would burn a tire when we got near it. We had some radio contact with whomever it was on the ground in Columbia. But it was very bad English and we didn't understand one another. I think we called the guy Paco, if I am not mistaken. We had difficulty locating it. As it turned out Columbia, it seems to me, has an overabundance of strips. Seems like everybody burned tires. It was kind of difficult. Fortunately, whomever was on the ground saw us and kind of gave us directions." They taxied in and turned the airplane around. Shortly, a tractor came loaded with duffel bags, the plane was refueled, oil changed, and they were gone.

They called "Short Stop" in Belize. "When we got across the coastline it was dark and when we made radio contact, they lit the field and it stuck out like a sore thumb." They landed, refueled and took off in no more than 25 minutes, headed for Alabama. Bagalman used the High Frequency Radio to talk to the people in Alabama. When they got close, he used the two-meter radio and spoke to "Home Plate" and Lynn. "When the plane landed in Alabama -- first of all they turned on the generators and had what looked like floodlights. It was pretty bright and pretty easy to land at this particular strip. We pulled up to the end of runway, got out of the airplane. And generally Dick and Rick would both be at the location, unload the duffel bags, put a few gallons, ten or fifteen gallons of fuel in the airplane. There were several other people on the ground, which I did not know at that time, and exchanged a few hellos/good-byes, and Fred and I would depart."

A month later, they flew another trip without any major hitches, but, not so the third trip. "When we landed, Fred lost control of the airplane and it swayed over and caught the brush. We pulled out of it, and ended up getting to the end of the runway. We examined the airplane when we came to a stop, the leading edge of the wing was dented pretty bad and the landing gear looked a little bent, a couple of fuel cells had been punctured or damaged, but it looked flyable. So we refueled it and flew it out of there." That was only the beginning of the nightmare.

They lost the auto-pilot en route. "We had to fight with the airplane the whole way back." When they finally arrived, they discovered that they had trouble getting the landing gear down. "We made our radio contact. And when we were lining up for our landing, which would have been the grass strip again, the gear wouldn't come down. It was jammed. And we tried on several occasions to get it down. And Fred started making comments about making a belly landing. That did not really thrill me a whole bunch. We really didn't have a lot of alternatives. We didn't have a great deal of fuel. For whatever reason, he tried the gear one more time and out it came and he landed the airplane."

Bagalman and Hartley flew the next trip in late May or June of 1986. Some time after refueling in Belize, another nightmare. "We had a problem getting airborne. The airplane lost attitude, airspeed, and actually we sat there and thought we were going to crash. And again for whatever reason that didn't happen and airspeed built up, altitude built up, and to Alabama we were coming." They made it to Alabama only to run into more problems. "We took the same route that we had always taken, west of New Orleans and on up north. A fog had come in. Very, very dense fog. We tried a couple of approaches and it was just -- Just could not land the airplane. We were circling for awhile hoping maybe it would break. The alternate airport would be the grass strip just right across the river. Well, that was fogged in too." They tried the Demopolis Airport itself. "I was talking to Dick and he was telling me how he could see up fifty or a hundred feet. That was all Fred needed to hear. He said he could get under it and make a landing anyway. We made a couple of approaches, but we didn't get that close. We left that airport."

They broke the bad news to Lynn, "We did not have a great deal of fuel. We had just about enough to get back to New Orleans. And our plan, what Fred and I planned to do, was to land the airplane in New Orleans and hope nobody went up to it, and get it out of there first thing in the morning." But on the way back they spotted an airstrip. "A really strange kind of thing happened. What we would do when we approached the Demopolis area, I would destroy the radio frequencies. For example, toss them out the window. Just get rid of stuff in the event we were seized, we wouldn't have all this stuff on board. I would erase all the programs for the radio and for the Loran. And whatever written notes I had, I would toss out of the window. And when we left the Demopolis area on the way back to New Orleans, just by happenstance we saw a little airstrip off the left wing. We circled it and it looked really quiet and we landed there. We ended up in Waynesboro, Mississippi."

"We were going to take -- unload the airplane. It was in these big duffel bags, but they were pretty heavy. Like seventy or eighty pounds. We tried to carry them to a fenced area off the airport. We made one trip, and then there was no way we could physically carry the stuff that far. We dumped it on the side of the runway and left. Now we had a dilemma. We did not have enough fuel to go back to Demopolis and we couldn't raise them on the two-meter radio. We didn't have the frequencies on the high-frequency radios anymore. We didn't have a choice. We went to New Orleans."

The next trip occurred within a few weeks or a month of the Waynesboro trip, in June or July of 1986 and, it too, involved a mishap. "When we were leaving Belize, Fred slipped off the runway and the plane was thrown into the trees and crashed. And I was sitting there wondering if it was going to catch on fire like you see in the movies. That evidently wasn't happening. We got out of the airplane. The load was taken off of the airplane. The airplane was burned to avoid detection." Hartley and Bagalman were smuggled into Mexico, from where they bought a ticket to Miami. They later returned to Belize, retrieved the load and delivered it to Demopolis.

Chapter 18
Kevin

Wood had earned every iota of the deprecation that he weathered on the stand. He had been arrogant, condescending and flippant, even to Bedwell. But Bronis and Black are great lawyers who are used to dealing with recalcitrant and malevolent witnesses. And they weren't strangers to the legend and lore of the Miami dope trade. It may not be true today, but in 1989 the Miami criminal defense bar was as inbred as Cain and Abel's cousins, something that this case illustrates. Information was cross-pollinated through former and current clients and by the same private investigators that they all used. Miami was then still a smallish city and they all hung out at the same bars and told each other war stories. Black and Bronis had cut their teeth as federal defenders and now they, or their friends, partners or associates, represented many of the same players back home.

And there was also plenty of real fodder. Woody had testified in another trial, had been recorded by undercover agents in numerous dirty dealings, and, just like in a divorce, each party knew all of the dirty details and wanted revenge for the other's unfaithfulness. Bronis' dogged, relentless, and blistering questioning took a heavy toll on Wood. Bronis was the sledgehammer that cracked Wood's cold facade and Black was the scalpel that cut out whatever little sinew remained. Together, they essentially eviscerated Wood and he came to acknowledge every sordid detail of his dirty dealings: the incident with the kidnap of the young boys, the tons of marijuana and coke that he had imported into the Keys, his constant working of the system even while he was incarcerated, his attempts to bribe government officials or manipulate other witnesses, the massive amounts of money that he made, the countless distributions throughout the country, and his association with the Colombian cartels.

And, since he had been handsomely rewarded for his testimony - he was not prosecuted in either Alabama district, his sentence in his current convictions would be lowered, and there was even the prospect of even more future consideration - he could be discounted as completely self-serving and questionable. "Yes," he acknowledged to Bronis, he was a "stern negotiator" and it was obvious that he had cut himself a sweet deal.

Save for his orange prison jumpsuit, Kevin Sheehy had all the visceral trappings of opportunity. He was a young, good-looking and obviously well-bred man. The room was awash in silent anticipation as what promised to be another important witness took the stand. And as he did, Sheehy plaintively looked at Lynn and began to cry. "Dickie, forgive me. I don't want to do this. They're making me do this," he trembled and wept, begging forgiveness from his best friend for this betrayal. This prologue to his testimony was devastating. It was at once human and self-authenticating. No other moment in the trial was more poignant than this Judas kiss. Or Lynn's Barabbas moment. Sheehy's heart-rending sobs and entreaties were met by a cold and icy stare, a disgusted steely-faced countenance that dripped with disdain. It nailed Lynn and made him look like the beast Bedwell claimed he was.

Kevin also had every reason in the world to jump through the government's hoops. He had a big hill to climb. His Mobile lawyer Rick Yelverton probably filled him in. Judge Butler's sympathies would not be with someone who had been active in smuggling and had gone to prison in 1985. If he faced her as a defendant Bedwell would no doubt bring up his past escapades. He had flown a load in from Jamaica and had been chased by Customs planes all the way from the Bahamas. He had made an emergency landing on a Florida airstrip and then placed an obstruction on the runway, nearly causing, the government had then maintained, a disaster for the agents that had been chasing him. Even the irony of it must've weighed on Sheehy. His timing couldn't have been more unfortunate. He had been in jail from 1985 and in a halfway house in Miami until July 30,

1987. Sheehy's first involvement after his release was on September 25, 1987, the importation that resulted in the crash that killed the Hartley brothers. He would do only one more and then be caught up in this.

A standard closing argument allegory that is used by criminal defense lawyers in describing the credibility to be attached to the testimony of a turncoat witness is the "Brave and the Snake" story. A Native-American Brave finds a snake freezing in the snow. "Help me," the snake says. "I am dying. Please take me into your tepee and warm me by the fire." "No, you'll bite me," he responds. But, being naive, he relents. He takes the snake into the tepee. The snake warms by the fire and, having recovered, bites him. When he is admonished by the Brave for the treachery, the snake replies "You knew I was a snake." Having told his or her parable, the criminal lawyer then sets out all of the reasons a jury should have a reasonable doubt about the turncoat witness. As with the others, the defense lawyers brought out all of Sheehy's past sins as reasons to doubt his credibility.

But, there's another corollary to the story. It is the perennial question in a criminal case, if the witness is as scummy as you defense lawyers make him out to be, why is he your best friend? Sheehy had real *bona fides* and even his sins painted the others with the same brush. He was two or three years younger but had known Lynn, Deshaw, and Eyster since childhood and Jack Marshall since high school. A diabetic, he was always compensating. His father had been the English teacher. Kevin was especially close to Ricou and his parents. His mother and father had died while he was young and they had looked after him like a son. When he had been a fugitive, they had risked prosecution by going to visit him in Austria. He had smuggled marijuana and cocaine with Lynn in the early 80s and was one of the members of their inner circle. "He always wanted to be a smuggler," according to Lynn.

It was the many personal favors that the two had done for each other and the many things that they had survived together that made his story all the more credible. He had, of course, been intimately involved with Wood, Deshaw and Lynn's drug runs. He had flown marijuana with Deshaw from Jamaica and had flown a plane load of cocaine from South America to the Bahamas. And on that trip, when the boat captain chickened out, Wood had hired him to finish the job and he and Lynn piloted the boat back. In 1987, Lynn hired him as an offloader for the Demopolis run.

These guys had been through a lot together. Sheehy had also been incarcerated at Eglin. When he got caught sneaking visits with his wife and was about to be indicted for escape and bribery, he went on the lam. It had been Lynn who helped him escape to Austria. Dickie took Kevin to the Bahamas by boat. Lynn had money squirreled away in Switzerland and helped him out. He had even gone back to the Bahamas to sneak Sheehy and his wife back into the country. He set them up in a residence in Alabama, bought them vehicles, etc.

The others, too, had given him money and taken care of his family. They always had each other's backs. One time in Jamaica, their plane had come under attack from bandits and Ricou barely made it out of there. Sheehy, stranded in the jungle spent a terror-filled night with the locals taunting him that they knew where he was and that they were coming to get him. But the next day, Ricou loyally returned. Dickie's dad died in a car wreck during their senior year in high school. It had been Kevin and Ricou who nursed their emotionally-fractured friend back to health.

These guys were solid with each other. But it was his Hobson's choice; betray your friends or go to jail. Kevin had tried being a standup guy before and what did it get him? He had gone to jail for contempt for refusing to testify in the Tampa case. Six months. It seemed like a better deal than ratting out your partner. They brought him before a grand jury. Still, he refused. They granted him immunity. No way. Then they indicted him for obstruction. He had learned who makes the rules. It's the Feds' Way or the highway, or in this case, prison for EVER.

The ghost of the Hartley boys haunted the trial. A fascinating end piece to what was, in total, a labyrinthian epic tale, Sheehy added even more first-person details. "Dickie told him it was foggy, that it might be hard for him to land. We didn't hear from him for a minute and he called back and said 'I've got – – I can see you, see the strip and everything.' We had a special high-powered light that would wield real strong. It was special made. We were worried about the pilot's safety, you know, because it was foggy. So we called back and we asked him. Dickie said 'It's foggy and we've got this light.' You know, we suggested 'Why don't you use it?' He said 'No, no, no. I got it, I got it. Don't talk to me anymore.' So we didn't talk to him anymore."

Sheehy described hearing the plane fly over and start his approach. There was a boom and the sky lit up, he said. "Well, we pretty much knew what had happened. So we all jumped in the van and we raced down there as fast as we could see if we could help them, see if we could save them. We saw wreckage strung across the road and little fires burning everywhere. There wasn't much left of the plane so there wasn't any doubt that there wasn't anybody alive on it. They couldn't have lived through it, it was so bad. We went down there to see if we could do something. We turned around. We went out the side gate. It was locked. We just pushed it open. We went back to the camp."

He may have avoided having all of his past sins exploited by Bedwell but that didn't keep the defense from going there. They brought up every one of Kevin's misdeeds, his many connections to Wood that had nothing to do with Dickie, Ricou or Bobby, and highlighted the many reasons to disbelieve anything he said. But, most importantly, as with the others, they used his testimony to contradict the testimony of his testifying cohorts.

Apart from the death of the pilots, there had really been no real violence associated with this group. But there was plenty of loose talk about it throughout the trial. The government constantly interjected testimony about guns, explosives and intrigues that involved doing bodily harm to others. Wood, for example, had testified that on one of the dope runs a student pilot had been on the field and was holding things up. Marshall, he said, had been prepared, on Dickie's orders, to take out the plane. Sheehy flatly contradicted that testimony, insisting that there had been no threats at all. It had not even been contemplated nor discussed. "No, and that would have been out of the question," Sheehy answered. That, he said, was a total lie.

Black continued his theme. Wood was large and in charge when it came to criminal activities, was he not? Sheehy agreed. Wood ran a huge organization and had been involved in many criminal activities and Sheehy had worked directly for him. "I worked for Mr. Wood several times. I'd say probably four to six or more." "I take it Mr. Wood is a fairly clever fellow, is he not?" "To say the least," Kevin said. "Wood is not a fellow who would want to voluntarily go to jail, would he?" "Not at all." And, although Butler did not allow Sheehy to answer whether or not he thought Wood was willing to lie to keep himself out of jail, no one doubted that he was.

Bronis peppered Sheehy with inside facts and tidbits from his and Woody's prior drug deals. He showed Kevin's intimate involvement with "his boss" and what Bronis repeatedly characterized as the "William Wood racketeering organization." And, as he ran down the many incidents in which the two of them had been involved, Kevin, also, would contradict Woody's testimony. "So, it would be untrue if your boss William Wood stated that in the spring of 85, in June of 85, you imported marijuana with David Jimenez from Andros Island to the Florida Keys?" "That would be incorrect," Sheehy responded.

Chapter 19
Another Insider

Hilery Deweese also met Lynn while at Eglin. After prison, Deweese went back home to the Keys and went back to running fishing charters. He had a commercial fishing scheme that required a $30,000 investment and Dickie lent it to him. It went belly up. He asked Dickie to let him work to pay it off and here he was, another group lieutenant corroborating what was by now the three main trunk lines of the government's story; the fatal crash, Clark's cowboy hijinks, and the abandoned load at Waynesboro.

On the night of the crash he had been "Side Door," had noticed the fog starting to form and reported it to "Home Plate." Then the blue van with the fuel arrived. So, too, the crew's black Suburban. The plane made contact. The plan, like the fog, had fatalistically come together. He witnessed the pilot's approach. Saw him pull away. "He couldn't see the lights but he was going to look again. He made another approach to the airport and still didn't land. Mr. Lynn called him on the radio and said 'It is clear down at this end, I can see the stars. Why don't you come down here?' Mr. Hartley said 'Don't worry about it. I have somebody riding with me. It will be okay' or something like that. The plane sounded as if it were in a working turn, the engines were not laboring but they were – something known as "fine pitch" and the engines were definitely turning more than the normal RPMs. And then I heard a clattering sound and then immediately after that a crunch and as I looked toward the end of the runway that he was trying his approach on, I saw a very brief pink flash in the fog. I believe I was the first one that spoke and I said 'He has crashed.' Mr. Lynn said on the radio, 'Oh, no.'"

They drove hellbent down the industrial road. Lynn radioed. "We can't get out here." Hilery told him to come back towards him to see if one of the gates was unlocked. It wasn't. They backtracked again, crashed through the little personnel gate and sped out. They picked up the other lookout and headed back to Purvis' camp. This night there was no celebration, just a very sad group of people. It was dead quiet, except when Kevin Sheehy mentioned that someone should go back out to see what could be salvaged and he and Purvis almost got into it. Deweese packed the radio equipment into the Suburban and headed out of there towards Nashville.

Deweese also put into context how it came about that they abandoned a load of cocaine in Mississippi. "It was about three o'clock, I guess. The plane was in contact and he verified it was very foggy. He made two attempts to land and couldn't find the runway. Mr. Lynn instructed him on the radio to fly the plane back to New Orleans and park it on the ramp, pull the curtains on it and if there was no trouble he would contact Snoopy tomorrow or the next day and we would arrange to bring it on the next night."

The next morning, Deweese said, they were on their way to Mississippi. "Mr. Lynn went to a phone and when he came back he was -- he said something about darn fools had left the cocaine on an airstrip in Mississippi and that instead of flying it back to New Orleans and that we ought to go see if we could recover it." But it was not meant to be. "As we went through the town we each had radios so we could communicate. I believe Dickie told Jack and Steve to wait at a restaurant we had passed and we would go out and see what the situation was and see what needed to be done and we would be back in contact with them. We drove on out to the airport at Waynesboro, which I recall being on the southeast side of town. On the way out there, right before we got to the sign that pointed off and said 'airport', we were passed by two state patrol cars at a high rate of speed with their emergency lights on and sirens going."

We turned down the access road and on that we were passed by another one. As we drove where we could see the airport or the airport buildings, there was a large number of, well, eight or ten, people grouped around a policeman who was on a pay phone and at that time another law enforcement car came past us, I think a city car. We could pretty well determine what had happened and we turned around and left. As we went through Waynesboro, we contacted Jack and Steve and all of us proceeded back to the camp. We went home."

The night of Bob's cowboy fiasco at Vaiden Field, it was a cold, wet, misty, rainy night, "probably one of the darkest nights I ever saw." The venue had changed. Sheehy had been arrested at Purvis' camp and the heat was definitely on. Now it was to be Vaiden Field. Deweese had gotten there just as it turned dark. New place, crappy weather, and a long wait. At about 2:00 in the morning, the Suburban and the S-10 came on the strip but there was still no word from the pilot. "Well, probably a half-hour to forty-five minutes later Mr. Lynn, I believe, had contact with the aircraft and Bob Clark stated that one of their pieces of navigation equipment had failed on them and they were not going to be able to come directly."

Clark could only guess how far away he was. "He said if we are right, we are twenty-six minutes away and I only have a hundred pounds of fuel." When he finally recognized Demopolis he asked for lights. The landing lights at the field were supposed to engage whenever an aircraft radio was keyed to a certain frequency. They weren't working. "I don't know where you are, I need some light," Clark yelled. The ground crew flashed their spotlight. It lit up the sky. And, if that wasn't enough to attract attention, the field's lights decided to come on too.

The aircraft had been on the ground no more than five minutes when the radioman picked up the police chatter. "Mr. Eyster came on the radio and said someone has reported lights on the airstrip. They are sending some law enforcement out to check on it." The Suburban wheeled out. "Side door" warned that a full-sized Ford was hauling ass down the road. It turned into the access road. Hilery, now frozen at his lookout position at the gate on the east side of the entrance road, saw it zoom into the airport. "The car turned in to the access road and came by me where I was at the gate over on the right side of the gate, over on the east side of the entrance road and proceeded into the airport." Then two more cars came in.

He had no doubt they were in deep yogurt. He could see their emergency lights. It was all he could do to force himself to breathe. They set up right there, oh so very close to where he was. "Two of them stopped at the gate about twenty feet from where I was and I turned my radio off because I was afraid someone would call me and the people in the cars, they were evidently outside of their cars talking, would hear the radio." He waited for what seemed eternity. But when a large hunting truck, big tires, loud muffler, joined the cop stakeout, he left to look for Barclay. He turned on his radio and called the others to warn them but no one answered. "I heard the aircraft engines start and pushed, evidently to full power. And then I observed the aircraft, with all of its landing lights on, taking off and it did take off and departed." He was now completely alone.

He found Barclay and they set out, blundering around in the muck. "It was muddy and had been raining and very muddy and your feet picked up twenty pounds of mud a piece." They climbed fences, avoiding houses, making sure they didn't rile up any dogs, and, finally, finally, finally, found the comfort of the dry hard highway. They broke off into two groups. Deweese and Barclay had been slowing the others down and had been left behind. Now on the road, they tried to contact someone. No one answered their May Days. Finally, they heard something and it was even more unsettling. Everyone was heading out.

Then, the helicopter. "About an hour had passed, a helicopter showed up with a big light and for that reason we stayed far off the road thinking that possibly they would be looking over the area." They found some high ground from where they could watch the highway intersection and kept up their futile effort to reach someone. Purvis' call came like a last-minute Governor's Death Row reprieve. He was at the camp trying to get one of the vehicles to work. Deweese told him what the radioman had said earlier, that the cops were looking for a pickup truck with cab lights. Purvis, God love him, called back. "They were coming to get us. They told us which vehicle. There was other vehicles occasionally on the road which they would be and that they would blink their lights." They did as he told them, hugged the road and the fence row waiting for his blinking light. He picked them up and they headed home.

Chapter 20

The Scent Gets Stronger

Ed Odom muses how plain and simple things can be in hindsight. "I was already involved in the case and didn't know it." He got a call from an old high school buddy. The man owned a crop dusting service in Grand Bay, a town in Mobile County and wanted to talk, but in person. Ed drove out to talk to him. "Two guys came here today to see me. One of them is named Tom McVea. I used to sky dive with him. I haven't seen him in a long time. He's out of Louisiana. Tom says to me 'I need some help. I'm involved with this group that is bringing in large quantities of cocaine and the airstrip we were using is hot. We can't use it anymore."

Odom wondered. ("Waynesboro?") McVea, his friend told him, had a proposition, "I want you to get me a strip down here that we can use and you will be paid for that." Odom collected the minutia that made for the dots he would only much later connect. They were flying a Panther Navajo, he was told. One of the principals was named "Marks Bagal or something like that" and used to "fly for the governor of Louisiana." He went back to DEA and started poking around. He found Marks Bagalman in the system and McVea's connection to a Panther Navajo. Bagalman had put it in McVea's name without him knowing it. Odom started watching the plane.

At just about the same time, one of Odom's Trooper's called him with what he thought was fishy business. It would turn out to be another piece of the puzzle. Assigned to a stolen car unit in North Alabama, he started filling him in. A landowner in Demopolis had been flying around looking at his land and noticed a bunch of cars out at a hunting camp. Not the typical beat up old trucks, trailers and SUVs, mind you, but late-model vehicles, fancy cars. "What," he queried the Trooper, "is going on here?" Guessing it was a hot car ring operating out of the hunting camp, the officer contacted the District Attorney's Office and they started an investigation. They went out to inspect the land but the cars were all gone. They saw a Black SUV with Alabama plates and a boat and trailer with Florida tags. The SUV's plates turned were bogus. But the trailer was registered to R.J. Lynn Construction Company in Tavernier Florida. There was a smuggler named Richard Joseph Lynn in the system.

When the crash happened everything came into perfect focus for Odom. He found the airplane's bill of sale in the wreckage and it was connected to Bagalman. The instrument panel had landed in the woods and on it was stuck one of those plastic embossed Dymo tapes, put there so that the pilot could remember the tail number. It was the Panther Navajo he had been watching. "I had two bodies and it turns out that one of them was the guy that was with Tom McVea. We sent the bodies to Forensics in Tuscaloosa. They called us back and they said that they needed dental records. I happened to be in Demopolis a day later when a guy calls from Louisiana and he says he thought that they were his brothers-in-law." Odom got the dentist's name and they confirmed that it was Fred and Joe Hartley. They went to Louisiana to confirm their identities, bringing along some of the personal effects from the crash. One of them was Joe Hartley's watch. Joe Hartley's girlfriend was wearing the matching watch. The picture was coming together but they still had to get enough to make a case. And, against who?

Almost a year passed. Odom got a call. "I just got in bed at the house when they called me and told me that they just had a smuggling incident at Vaiden Field. Everybody and his brother headed up there. I sent one of my guys from Selma and headed up there. It was cold as hell that night. The guy that runs the airstrip says 'I know aircraft. The aircraft that took off was a 400 series Cessna.'" Odom puts out the BOLO, specifying the special importance of the type of aircraft. "While I'm standing on the strip at Vaiden Field, I get a call saying that a 400 series Cessna had landed in Muscle Shoals. I get Bobby Brown out there and he traces him all over."

Most prosecutions are about putting the facts together after the fact. This was not what is called a "dry conspiracy." There was plenty of dope. They had the dope from the crash and the dope from Waynesboro. But it was, as was characterized by one of the defense lawyers at the Miami detention hearing, pretty much a historical case. It's much better if you actually catch them in the act, so the feds took a proactive role, infiltrating the organization through the pilots Clark and Abbott and Chambless, Lynn's man in Alabama.

Scared out of their wits, Clark and Abbott had cut a deal and that included playing spy. It was probably the smartest thing that they have ever done. When Brown had stopped them at Muscle Shoals, he had engaged in a tactic commonly used by the police, killing them with kindness, assuring them graciously that he just wanted to clear some things up and asking them if they minded answering a few questions. They had flown from Tampa where the plane had been bought by someone and they were delivering it, Abbott said. Brown never asked them about Vaiden Field or why they had used false names or why Clark had lost his pilot's license. He just took it all in like Andy of Mayberry. He asked for and was given permission to copy the contents of their wallets, which he sent to Odom. Steve Purvis' business card was in there. Steve Purvis was cross-referenced to Richard J. Lynn in the DEA database.

The pilots began making undercover tapes. On them the participants discussed past deals and were planning more trips. Agents followed Clark and Abbott. They took pictures, effected surveillance, got hotel receipts and the hundreds of other mundane tasks that go into preparing a prosecution. It was not for nothing that Clark and Abbott had been offered complete immunity, something that would mean a lot to a two-time loser like Clark. Not only did the government have yet another pilot and chief conspirator, they were getting direct corroboration and had a proactive case.

And a witness to explain it all. Clark told the jury that he and Lynn had been incarcerated together at Eglin and had run into each other accidentally at a Miami airport. Some time later, Lynn called him and asked him to come to the Keys to talk. Deweese, who he recognized from Eglin, was at the meeting. They wanted him to fly for them. Lynn was moving to Colorado, leaving Deweese and Steve Purvis to arrange the loads. To finalize the deal, Clark traveled to Miami to meet Pruna. He would get $400,000 and his copilot, would get $150,000.

Clark, Deweese and Purvis then flew to New Orleans to meet Hartley and to get grounded in the realities of the trip, the route, the procedures, and communications. They would also get to see the plane and the landing strip. "I asked Fred if this 88 line that I had been told about was a safe entry point in his opinion and he said, 'Well, of course, I have flown it seventeen times.' And I discussed all one would need to know to get into the United States. He told me that he had flown in at 3,500 feet, sometimes 1,500 feet but if I stayed at 1,200 to 1,500 feet, things would be fine."

After Abbott returned from Belize where he had been checking the different airstrips and security, the two of them flew to Colombia, returning with 600 kilograms of cocaine. Pruna, Purvis and Marshall left with the cocaine, and Abbott and Clark refueled the plane themselves. Things rocked on rather uneventfully for awhile and they made one or two more trips. In early September of 1987, Abbott traveled back to Belize to see a new airstrip and get ready for another trip, really a series of seven trips with each flight crew alternating. He returned to Miami, where he reported back to Clark. "It would have been an intermediate type or dirt road which they had widened for a little more than a mile to about sixty feet wide rather than the average width of the road But it was just basically a road out in the middle of nowhere." That smuggling trip was cancelled, however, but only because there was a hurricane in the Gulf.

A week or so later, Abbott and Clark returned to Miami to make another attempt at the trip. "I had decided that it was rather foolish to depart at 5:30 or 6:00 without knowing whether Fred got on the ground safely or not. So I had delayed our trip already for a day. I was going to depart, instead of the first morning, the second morning. And nobody came to pick us up. It was going to be Eddie. And it got seven, eight, nine o'clock and we hadn't heard anything and I was getting a little nervous and so was Pat and we were about ready to leave when we got a phone call from Andy. He didn't explain anything. He just said 'The worse has happened.' And I never in my life thought or dreamed Fred would crash because he was a very competent pilot, I was told."

The dangerous conditions in Belize were not acceptable and the pilots were complaining. The Hartley crash was followed by another crash and yet another trip to salvage the load. "I told Dickie on several occasions that after this June trip that quite different arrangements would have to be made because I would not go down to Belize again and land on a cane road." Clark laid out his reasons. "Narrow, wet possibly. There is no sense, in my opinion, taking a chance getting that far and destroying yourself or the aircraft because we had already, if the aircraft crashed, we had already seen an incident in the previous December where things do go wrong rapidly."

They started looking at a plane that could make the trip all the way from Columbia, a Titan Cessna 404. They took the same route over Great Inagua, Haiti, down to Colombia, south of Barranquilla, and picked up 600 kilograms of cocaine. They headed north, this time avoiding Belize. They flew over Swan Island and then due west to a point where we would stay well clear of Cuba and then cut northwest in the vicinity of Cancun and Cozumel and picked up the 88 line and flew into US airspace at 800 foot altitude. They headed to Vaiden Field, which is about 30 miles east of Demopolis.

Unfamiliar with the new plane, they had loaded the cargo inefficiently and had to wildly correct for their mistake. It was also causing havoc with the navigation system. "We had a few problems finding it because we knew the Omega was off but didn't know which way east or west and the Loran wasn't working." They were low on fuel and didn't know where they were. They got on the high-frequency and the two-meter radios. "We indicated that we were pretty low on fuel and we needed to come direct. They had a spotlight that they were shining up in the air which we didn't see it until we got a couple of miles away." The load crew came in and the coke was gone in minutes. They started refueling the plane.

That's when the cops came. "Well, Steve had an electric pump and we got about a hundred gallons from him and Deke had about a five-gallon pail and we got about 30 gallons from him. And just as I guess Steve's tank, a 100-gallon tank that was in back of a pickup, emptied, Hilery called us from the main gate and said that there were three troopers coming in. I had just closed the -- put the fuel tank cap on the right wing and Steve said he was out of gas when we heard that call. So I put the other one on, the tank on the left wing. And just as I walked around the corner of the wing, I looked down the runway and there were troopers headed down the runway."

Clark jumped in the airplane and closed the door. "As I was sitting down, all the switches are on the panel right by your left leg in the Cessna and I just hit what I thought was all the switches and fortunately it started immediately. And I didn't know where I was on the runway. I knew that I had landed one way to the northwest that I could turn around and make it the other way and so I added quite a bit of power on the right side and turned the aircraft around real fast. And when I hit all of those switches, I hit the lights. So I had lights on and they had lights on and they headed for me and I headed for them and then we kind of headed away from each other as I broke ground." They headed towards Huntsville where they were eventually interrogated.

Chapter 21
Backup

Some of the undercover conversations made by Clark - like the discussion about sending Marshall to "deal with" Bagalman and the investigative reports that discussed Chambless, "Bobby" and others - sounded like real threats. But they were vague or ambiguous comments, open to interpretation, sounded like bluster and open to the obvious criticism that they were just prejudicial things put out there only to inflame the jury. Robert Wardle and Dave Davenport, former Special Forces military types who had been hired to perform security functions in Belize, however, put flesh on the bone. Their testimony, mostly anecdotal and outrageous, added Black Ops overtones to the picture Bedwell was trying to paint that Lynn and his Key West friends weren't some sort of romantic Jimmy Buffett pirates but were really bad dudes.

Their testimony underscored the seamy underbelly of the drug trade and injected all manner of intrigues and adventures, most of it occurring in Belize and having little to do with Lynn. They had been connected as trainers to Mitch Werbell, the notorious arms dealer who ran some sort of nutcake school for assassins and political intrigue in Georgia. Davenport claimed that he had scored a case of C-4 explosives and was intending to send it to Belize. He had been arrested with an arsenal in his vehicle. He had shipped Wardle's M-16 to him so that he "could be familiar with his own weapon." Purvis gave the jury his assessment of Davenport as someone who would "do anything to enhance his condition as far as this trial is concerned" and characterized him as a liar. "I don't have much respect for the man." The government would later officially proclaim Davenport a liar. But during the trial he testified, saying that Lynn was concerned because Wood was testifying in Oklahoma and had offered Davenport $150,000 to find a "solution to the problem."

Wardle provided testimony about the Belize end of the enterprise, connecting Lynn and Pruna to it, and corroborating Clark. The sidekicks, Abbott and Davenport, provided corroborating testimony and exhibits like aeronautical charts of the locations of the strips in Belize, telephone bills, trip receipts and itineraries. They provided the interstices, filling in a lot for the jury of a very convoluted story that had a lot of moving parts. Freddie Pou had been a major player in the New Orleans part of the equation. He had been Wardle's Team Commander in Viet Nam and they had remained close friends. Wardle, along with Dave Davenport, another Viet vet, drove dope for Pou. When Freddie got wind that he was about to be indicted, he fled the country. That's when he became "Shortstop," the man in charge of the midpoint operations in Belize.

In the Summer of 1987, the three of them reconnected in Cancun. Pou, who now went by the name of Johnny Morales, introduced them to Lynn, Hartley, and Bagalman and told them what the deal was. They were building a new airstrip near the Mexican border. The Belizean Defense Force, the local police department, and the tactical unit, were all on the take. But refugees from El Salvador and Nicaragua were resorting to banditry and were becoming an ever increasing unknown. Pou needed someone who could help him control them, someone who knew their way around security. Wardle and Davenport would be their muscle, setting up a perimeter and running reconnaissance, for which they would each be paid $10,000 a load. They liked it. They did some preliminary reconnoitering and went back to wait on orders.

Five months later, Wardle was called to Cancun where Pou gave him a recap. They hadn't even remotely slowed down. A few days after their meeting, Clark and Abbott had brought a load into Demopolis. But in October, a load of cocaine crashed. They buried the plane. Secured the coke. Waited for another plane like forever and after lugging the load to the airfield for a few false starts - when the plane had finally, for real, made it - they were ambushed by bandits. The aircraft took a round in the nose. The nose wheel was blown out. One of the pilots and an offloader were wounded. The bandits took the load, 17 duffel bags, and drove off with it. At some point they couldn't carry them all and started caching them. Pou got a Guatemalan Indian tracker and they recovered 11 of the bags, secured them again. Here he was in Cancun hoping Wardle and Davenport could save his bacon. That $25,000 was starting to sound like a bargain. They needed to get those duffel bags out. Davenport and Wardle agreed to do it, collecting maps and Intel and, returned to Atlanta, to map out a plan before their return to Belize.

Wardle checked out the airstrip. He and the tracker who had recovered the 11 bags went into the bush for two days to figure out how the ambush had gone down, where the people had stayed, the number of people involved, avenues of approach, where they had RONed (remained over night) and from where and how they had set up their operation. Back at the strip, they formulated their Special Ops plan. They spread out their people. "We had determined that we had all the bases covered except for the bandits. And that was a question of maintaining a deterrent, which is basically running a 'profile.' They know you're in the area. If anybody sees you they know you're there. We just kept checking and listening and using the Starlight scope."

Not that his plans sounded all that passive. "The only loophole that we thought was that if for some reason the payoff to the government people wasn't sufficient enough, they might come up the road. They don't fly their choppers at night down there. And so there was a bridge, and we were going to blow the bridge if the government came up, and then do an escape and evasion across the border."

Finally, the plane was en route from Haiti. The ground crew, now entirely new because the old crew had all been scared off by the ambush, arrived around midnight and were "inserted" onto the strip. "There were quite a number of people involved because the Orange Walk people didn't like to come back to that area to work because of the bandits." At early dusk, Pou went to the strip with some of the duffel bags that had been stashed at the safe house. He dug up the rest of the contraband from where it had been buried and brought the load to the strip. A fuel truck arrived. They were massed and ready, about 26 people, including 9 uniformed Belize Defense Force personnel. And Davenport, Wardle, and Pou.

The plane arrived, was turned, refueled, loaded, tail numbers changed, and sent on its way. After nearly six months of delays with the load, the aircraft took off with a ground time of no more than two hours. But the plane never made it. It either exploded - after all this is a load of cocaine with a fuel bladder sitting on top of it - or the crew ripped them off. Because the load had been lost in Belize and Pou could not travel to the US, it fell to Wardle to come to the States and explain what had happened. Wardle was starting to be more than the muscle. His testimony linked Lynn and Deweese to money payments to Pou, as well as giving an economic breakdown of the local costs involved in the operation. He corroborated what Clark and Abbott were saying.

The Belizean government, he said, had destroyed the new field. Pou, now had lost a load and had no location. He settled on a "hit and run" paradigm. They would use different locations and use them only once. They settled on a road cut through a sugar cane field. "On Saturday night the ground team inserted, and repairs were made on the strip and the cane was cut back away from the strip so the wings wouldn't catch on the sugar cane." He described for the jury how they waited, the mechanics like the lighting of the toilet paper rolls, the landing, refueling and meeting the pilot, Clark. Also a veteran, Clark had introduced himself and they had passed the time telling each other war stories until the plane was ready.

Chapter 22
Abbott

Patrick Abbott and Bob Clark became friends in Alaska where they had been bush pilots. Clark's wife was his child's godmother. They kept in touch and reconnected when they found themselves in Florida. It had been a shock to Abbott when Bob went to prison for drug smuggling. But things weren't going so well for Abbott either. One thing led to another and next thing you know, here he was sitting as second seat in a drug smuggling operation and, later, spilling his guts to the cops about it.

On the day of the incident there had been a lot of chatter coming over the two-meter radio about the police being on their way. Abbott heard Deweese's warning that the cops were rounding the corner and entering the airport area. Everybody scattered. Purvis drove into the woods. Abbott helped fly the plane into the blackness.

As Clark's co-pilot and main partner in crime, Abbott was tasked from the very start with making sure that they had their bases covered. He took care of the essentials. He flew to Miami and met with Hilery and Andy and from there he went to Belize to look at the strip and make sure the ground operations were adequate. He met Pou who took him on a tour of the airstrips located in the northern part of the country at Orange Walk. "The Queen," a roughly 5,000-foot long, 60-foot wide, gravel strip, sat like a pimple on the face of the Belizian jungle and was, Abbott thought, certainly adequate for their needs. But because the life expectancy of a field is short here, he was shown others. There was the "Sugar Factory," which was just a service road cut into the middle of a cane field, "Dog Leg," an open meadow in the jungle, and a farm in the Blue Creek Mennonite community. "That particular strip had been bombed by the BDF and had big holes in it, but they were willing to replace it as an alternate." Lighting was already makeshift, the burning toilet paper rolls, so he made sure that they knew how far apart to space them so the pilots could gauge distance and depth. Satisfied, Abbott returned and reported that they were good to go.

After a few days rest, he and Clark were flying to Colombia from Miami. Abbott was the navigator and radio man. As they hit different locations they would check in on the list of frequencies that Bob had been provided. "We were to have UHF (Ultra High Frequency) capabilities from the South Florida area at all times depending on altitude and weather. We had code names for Colombia to use and Belize to use and back at our eventual landing site, which was Demopolis, Alabama and the code names for that and frequencies. I had quite a few frequencies but I was supposed to talk to a channel that was to be called 'Red Baron'." In Columbia they used the two-meter radios, changing their frequencies often and using the code names of "Juliette" and "Romeo." They landed about 30 miles southeast of Barranquilla, helped load the plane, refueled and were back in the air within an hour and a half, headed for "The Queen."

They arrived at dusk and had no problem landing. On the ground in Belize, a man in a cowboy hat was holding two flashlights, guiding them to the end of the runway. They shut the aircraft down and pointed it in the same direction that it had landed. "A group of Belizians moved about us and pushed on the tail of the airplane and spun it around because it was a nose gear airplane. They then proceeded to refuel the aircraft. I sat and talked to Johnny and introduced him to Bob because Bob hadn't met him. I said hello to the other gentlemen, Pinto and Gato, who were supervising the crew. They taped our tail number on the tail so that on re-entry in, if we had a fly-along, they couldn't read our tail number. Johnny gave us a bucket of what he called Belizian fried chicken and sent us on our way."

They came over Mobile Bay flying at 500 feet, headed north. They landed and were met by Andy and Steve Purvis. "They were very jubilant, if you will. When I got out of the airplane, Steve Purvis come up and shook my hand and said 'congratulations' and I said 'thank you very much' and went about fueling the airplane." The black Suburban backed up to the back of the airplane, offloaded the coke and it was off the field within eight minutes. A half-hour later the plane was gone. Abbott had just made a cool $150,000.

Emboldened by the success of some of these trips, they decided to expand the number of flights. Bob called Abbott and told him to head for Miami. "They were talking about they had quite a few trips lined up. I believe it was seven that Fred and his copilot and Bob and I were going to do on an alternating basis." The first plane took off and they waited to take off the following day, but noone came to pick them up. They were worried. "I called my wife that night and she had heard about an airplane crash around the Demopolis area. We presumed something had gone wrong with Fred's trip but it was the following day that we were notified by Andy that Fred and his copilot had crashed." Not even Fred's death slowed them down. Andy was still looking for alternate landing strips and having Abbott look at new fields. They were still getting shipments into Alabama. Then the incident at Vaiden Field happened.

Chapter 23
Trial, An Error

Why did Dickie continue to deal dope? Towards the end of things, the refusal to accept a plea bargain to the CCE charge might have been reasonable and the ability to negotiate another deal might have been beyond his control, but why keep doing what you're doing when the playing field was littered with so many red flags that a blind man would have, at the very least, tripped over them. A car rental agent in Meridian had showed him a Customs Agent's business card and told him that he had been asking questions specifically about him. He was stopped coming back from Belize and knew that agents followed him in New Orleans. They lost the load in Waynesboro. A massive shipment of cocaine is news everywhere, much more so in rural Mississippi. And it seems that, at the very least, the crash that resulted in the death of his partner would have put him on notice that it was time to quit. The Customs reports that Jordan shared with them were right there in black and white and how more concrete a piece of evidence do you want than finding a transponder on your plane.

Hubris. "You get to the point where you start believing that you're bulletproof," he says, now older and wiser. And, he muses, he had even walked away from everything. He handed the business over to Purvis and Deweese and moved to Colorado. With six million dollars squirreled away, he and his family were hitting all of the skiing hot spots, headed west and then? Who knew? Tahiti, or wherever else they might fancy. Instead he let Hartley talk him back into the game. They were going to do a joint trip and really rake it in, but instead the whole thing came crashing down.

"We just started talking about skiing and hunting and he out of the blue said 'What are you doing?' I said, 'Nothing just hanging out with my wife and kids' and he said 'I'm bored to death, let's do one.' At first I just laughed but then he came back with 'My brother wants to fly with me so he will have his own money and right now he feels bad always asking me for it.' His brother was deathly scared of flying and I felt that a little funny but agreed to meet them in Miami the next day. Of course, I had to lie to my wife and do it on the sly. It turned out to be the worst decision I ever made for everyone concerned." He told his wife he was going hunting and set off for Miami.

Andy, a man with grand illusions, wanted to fly larger loads, flying two planes in tandem. "Basically the idea was to have one on it is way back and another one going. So that they could do a series of trips in a very short period of time," Bagalman would testify. The Hartleys and Clark and Abbott also flew to Miami. The plan stalled, however, when a hurricane started brewing. Dickie and the pilots holed up in a hotel. The tension was too much for Clark and Abbott. They booked. But on the third day, when the storm suddenly veered off into the Atlantic, Fred took it as an almost cosmic sign. "He said, 'Look at that. The storm turned. We're going.'" Dickie took Fred and Joe over to Tamiami Airport and sent them south.

He flew to Alabama where Purvis picked him up. Deweese, Sheehy, Eyster, and Barclay were already at the camp loading the gear. Dickie checked in with the midpoint at Belize. Freddie Pou, assured him that "it was all good." He joked that Joe had discarded a six-pack of dead Heinekens and commented that he needed it for his nerves since he hated to fly. The crew left the camp at about 1:30 in the morning and headed for the field. They drove to the end of the strip, broke out the night vision goggles, the radios and the rest of the equipment and started getting ready. Nothing seemed out of the ordinary. It was crystal clear and pleasant. Wondrous. Quiet. The primal woods majestic and lush. The air, also primordial, was faintly sensual and virginal and the sky rained down an accompanying symphony of Alabama stars. Dickie was seduced by it. He stretched out on the runway and, bathed by the caressing warmth of the previous day's sunshine that still emanated from the concrete, he soaked it all in.

He jumped when his radio squelched. That meant that the plane was about 40 miles out. He checked in with Fred who assured him that everything had gone smoothly and bragged about how well his brother had done. He told Dickie that he'd "see him in a few." Not too long after that, though, Hilery got on the radio. He reported the fog rolling in from the river. The assessment, that it was "not too bad," was passed along to Fred. Dickie asked him if he wanted to come in from the other direction, offering to move the ground crew. Fred checked it out. "He came by on his downwind and said 'Nah partner, I've got this. See you in a couple. No more talking.' I heard a very loud crack which I truly believe was them hitting the pines and then there was a huge fireball and I knew they were both dead."

Dickie jumped into the Suburban and sped to the crash scene. The plane, a fiery mess, was blocking the road. Sheehy suggested salvaging as much of the load as they could but this set Purvis and Dickie off. "It really pissed me off 'cause my best friend and his brother were laying there dead and he wanted to grab blood money as far as I was concerned. We turned around and I smashed through the gate in front of the FBO and we drove to the camp very heavy-hearted. We packed up quick as we could and then drove to New Orleans and caught a flight to Miami. I met with Andy and told him about the crash and it was very hard not to cry. I think he even cried. Then I jumped on a flight back to Colorado."

What about continuing after the crash? Lynn moved his family back to Sarasota where they lived under all sorts of aliases. "Clark had done three trips with Steve and Hilery, two for Andy and one for them. I met him in Tampa the day after we barely got away and had just lost the plane at Muscle Shoals and I said 'Well, that's it for me. I don't need this shit anymore.' He said 'Ah, man, shit like that happens. Let's do a couple more.' At first I was a little dumbfounded since he was always worried about the what ifs. I told him that I was finished and he said 'Oh come on man, don't leave me with these guys. They are really shaky and I need you there.' So, I went back to work but really couldn't understand why Clark wanted to work again after coming so close to getting caught at Vaiden Field. As it turned out he had a pass and completely different motive."

And a trial? In Mobile, Alabama? What was coming was no surprise. The voluminous discovery - the Customs ROIs (Reports of Investigation), DEA 6s and FBI 302s, etc. - spelled out what he already knew, that his closest friends were rolling on him and that the government had a mountain of corroborating evidence, including resources not explainable by anything approximating a real job. Those toys, millions of stashed dollars, and sensitive inside information were valuable bargaining chips. That's what Wood and Pruna did. He no doubt had some of this same type of information. After his sentencing Sheehy would go to the Bahamas where he provided testimony against some smugglers, was given a gracious "Her Majesty Thanks You" letter and a Rule 35 sentence reduction motion in the bargain. Given the sentence Lynn faced, why not deal? More hubris? Honor? Maybe. Was it, like dealing dope and playing freedom fighter, just another thrill?

The usual suspect would be Bedwell. Her offers are notoriously over-the-top. She is unflappable in her faith, legal and religious, and works at remaining uncorrupted by the ugliness of the dope world realities with which she deals. One of those realities is compromise. She sees it as a bitter pill she only begrudgingly swallows. Odom, however, blames Sessions' meddling and Bedwell's petulance for setting up a situation that still continues to haunt Lynn. The case in Alabama had been unique because part of it existed in the Northern District and part of it existed in the Southern District. And, like the boundary that demarcated them, a river of bad feelings would run between the sides charged with prosecuting the case. Not a raging river, perhaps, but a stream of discontent, resentment and jealousy. These internecine rivalries would come to compromise the case and in the end result in making fall guys of Lynn and Marshall, and quite possibly, Bedwell herself.

Organizational rivalry and politics are nothing new to prosecutions, especially federal prosecutions and even more so in such a high-profile case. Like it or not, a prosecutor's office is, at core, a political office run by people who often have side agendas and long memories. Like any other law enforcement organization, it counts its successes by the number and caliber of scalps it takes and the assets it seizes. Inter-agency animosity is another constant. The FBI, DEA, and Customs squabble with each other like siblings. They don't play well together and they don't like to share. This case had its arguable beginnings in at least two or three different places and involved Customs and the DEA. The case agent, although assigned to the DEA, was "just" an Alabama State Trooper. "I have a lot of badges but none of them say 'US.'" Almost immediately the districts and the agencies began jockeying for what was easily one of the juiciest cases to come along in quite some time. Maybe ever.

Wood's cocaine connection was Fabio Ochoa but during his debriefing he had also thrown Pablo Escobar's name into the mix. "I was supposed to meet him," he told the debriefers. Both names were high value targets. Escobar was sought worldwide as the head of the Medellin Cartel. Fabio Ochoa was his ruthless lieutenant. The agents and prosecutors had no way of knowing it at that point but it was a different Fabio Ochoa, not the one who had been implicated in Barry Seal's murder. The Southern District of Alabama has a special connection to the Seal issue. It had been DEA's treachery, some in Customs claimed, that had caused his death. Seal's execution in Baton Rouge by a Columbian hit squad had caused such a major rift that DEA agents left the agency and went to Customs. They created *Operation Skymaster* and headquartered a little cottage industry of undercover drug transportation in Mobile. Customs had hidden all of the operation's assets here. That included money in bank accounts, airplanes and snitches. They had an entire ring of reformed drug rogues scattered about nearby. Noriega's pilot lived in Fairhope. Seal's brother-in-law worked for them as a pilot. They hid him in nearby Mississippi. There were four or five of these guys living in Mobile, working side by side with Customs agents out of clandestine offices at Brookley Field.

Apart from being driven by the idea of taking down extremely high value targets, adding Pablo Escobar or Fabio Ochoa's name to the investigation had an important practical impact on the case. Running a governmental agency is just like running a household or business. Everything is competing against a budget. Like any budget, there is always something put aside for the big things. Investigative reports and information are collected and stored in the DEA's Investigative Reporting and Filing System (IFRS). "Violator identifiers" consist of Geographical Drug Enforcement Program (GDEP) codes and the Narcotics and Dangerous Drugs Information System (NADDIS) code numbers, the numbers assigned to drug violators and suspected drug violators and "entities that are of investigative interest." The GDEP code, is assigned to each case when the investigative file is opened. It indicates the classification of the violator, the types and amount of suspected drugs involved, the priority of the investigation and the suspected location and scope of criminal activity. Escobar's name in the GDEP code heightened the case's importance and freed up money from the penny pinchers. It meant a lot more leeway in what they could do, like investigative travel, expansive techniques like wire taps and transponders, and the authorization of additional man hours.

As it turns out, Escobar was, indeed, connected to this case, but what Wood threw out as a *bon mot* was chaff. It would not be until a year later, when the feds finally caught up with Jorge Valdes, that they had the true Escobar connection. But it is obvious from the debriefing recording that the questioners bit on Wood's gambit hook, line, and sinker. Having Escobar and Ochoa certainly was part of their calculus. Crush these guys and they'll lead us to the boss. Sessions, who had only recently survived a brutally unfair public offing, was probably feeling a bit less patient, a whole hell of a lot less charitable, and very politically queasy these days. His judicial appointment had been responsible for handing his beloved

Reagan Administration its first defeat, preceding the Bork debacle by nearly a year. Jefferson Beauregard Sessions, who would have his middle name repeated in much the same way as President Obama's - proof positive of some sort of foreshadowing of a hereditary character flaw - would be caught up in ridiculous accusations that he was an extra-special bigot. Two years later (and a few years before he would announce his successful candidacy for United States Senator), here he was, not just making the talking head announcement, but personally directing a prosecution three years in the making. The case touched other jurisdictions and countries. It had millions of dollars in assets ripe for forfeiture. The mix became explosive for intramural jealousies, posturing, and intrigues - real and imagined.

The jockeying began almost immediately and was exacerbated by the fact that Vaiden Field is in the Northern District and that Abbott and Clark had flown to Muscle Shoals which is also in the Northern District. After being contacted by their lawyer, the US Attorney's office in Birmingham set up a meeting there even though the bulk of the criminal activity and the law enforcement investigation had been in the Southern District. They informed the Mobile United States Attorney's office about it as a *fait accompli* and only as a matter of organizational protocol. But the Mobile United States Attorney's office has always been a player, especially in drug cases. Sessions and Odom went to Birmingham where an immunity deal, with Sessions' approval, was negotiated by the Northern District. "That's when it starts getting out of my hands. And Jeff Sessions, all of a sudden he's Sherlock Holmes. We go to Birmingham. Sessions and Joe McLain are there. They decide that we're going to give these two assholes immunity and I say 'Whoa! Why in the world would we do that? We got them nailed to the wall. We're not going to be able to arrest them today, but Jesus Christ, give me a break, cut a deal, but no immunity.' They go into the next room and the next thing I know they have immunity. It went downhill from there."

Odom's misgivings had been correct. In a subsequent debriefing, Purvis would contradict Clark and Abbott's numbers. He said that they had been paid much more. Purvis would know. He was a lieutenant. Odom reported this to Bedwell who is a hard-nosed and unforgiving prosecutor. Like her boss, she draws lines in the sand that quickly become indelible. She is completely ruthless and heartless with those that betray or cross her. When a witness is caught lying it has to be reported and the defense has to be told. It cheapens the value of a witness and that is one of her pet peeves. That she gave them another chance is puzzling. It certainly had something to do with their status as important government witnesses. They were so important that she had them safely ensconced in the Witness Protection Program. For whatever reason, she did it and they fessed up. The trial moved forward.

Recognizing the value of the case, Sessions was hot to get an indictment. As the boss, it was certainly his prerogative to put pressure on Odom to move the case faster, which he did. "I'm sitting in Jeff's office and he keeps saying 'This is a great case. We can really do some great things with this case but I'm really concerned about all of these people that we don't have identified. I think you need to speed up trying to identify them.' I laughed. I said, 'Jeff we're doing that every day.'" But when Sessions tells Odom, who is assigned as a task force agent to the DEA, that the FBI and Customs had both volunteered to take over the case, it laid open some of the sensitivities involved in the case. Odom exploded. "I'll get this case done. I don't need the goddamned FBI or Customs taking this case. They're not going to. Let's get something straight. Never in my life will I walk into your office and tell you or one of your people how to prosecute this case. You don't tell me how to investigate.' Weeks later he assigned Gloria to the case and I never had to deal with him again."

Odom claims that the indictment was another problem intrinsic to the case. "The indictment was one of the worst indictments I've seen in my life. We indicted Ricou Deshaw when he hadn't done shit in the Southern

District. We indicted marijuana stuff in there that had nothing to do with it whatsoever. All of that indictment was Sessions. He wrote it all. He presented me as a witness, I'm the only person to have testified before the grand jury and once the indictment was out he assigned an assistant to handle it and had nothing to do with it." McLain, who had been involved with the case, offered to assist Bedwell, according to Odom. "Joe [McLain] told Gloria 'I will come down and sit with you in the courtroom and help you with the case. You'll need help.'Jeff says, in my presence, when she broached the topic of Joe McLain coming down, he said 'No no, no, I'll help you prosecute the case.' He walked in the court room two times." As it turns out, it was one time too many.

"Dickie Lynn himself would've cooperated in this case and could've done a world of good. Sessions says to me 'When you arrest him, you tell him he's got one opportunity to cooperate and that's to... immediately...When you arrest him he has to tell you 'yes' or 'no' and if he says 'no' or if he doesn't cooperate then there will be no cooperation." When Odom arrested Dickie in Sarasota he told Lynn what Sessions had said. "He says to me 'Ed, I don't know if there's anything I can do to help you but I've got to talk to my attorney first. I said 'I understand that, but you keep this in mind, there is absolutely nothing you can do to help me. We're talking about helping you." Subsequent attempts to negotiate a plea proved unsuccessful. "Roy Black told me that he sat down with Jeff and told him what his guy could do for him and Jeff offered to let him plead guilty to Count 1 and dismiss all of the counts of the indictment." Count 1 was the CCE, which carried an automatic life sentence. "Black told Jeff, 'That's stupid. Why would we do that? I'll take my chances in court before I do that' and Jeff said 'That's the only deal you'll get from me.'"

Later, with Escobar and a corrupt Florida sheriff now in her radar, Bedwell revisited the idea of a plea but still insisted on the CCE plea with only the promise of a possibly lesser sentence if later he was deemed to have "substantially cooperated." Dickie rejected that offer. "Of course I'd have to tell on all of those I never would've thought would tell on me. My thoughts were to hang tough for my guys. And a life sentence didn't seem like such a deal, especially since Pablo had killed his share of cooperators and I had my family to worry about."

The trial ended on October 17, 1989. It had lasted five weeks. Having spent so much time together, the jury, judge, agents, lawyers and even some of the defendants, had developed a camaraderie. Everyone, it seemed, had reached their personal assessments of the character of the defendants, the lawyers, the agents and the witnesses. The professional and courteous respect that the agents and defense lawyers had for each other during their interplay was obvious and uncharacteristic. Black's understatement, Lazzara's grace and Bronis' aggression had made mostly fans and the defense had successfully laid out the bare reality that the charges were very serious, the sentences would be draconian and that the character of some of the government witnesses was seriously in question. Bedwell had represented the United States admirably, leaving everyone with a somewhat accurate picture of what was truly a very complex case.

The jury? It took its responsibilities very seriously, delivering what was, in essence, Solomon's half baby. They had deliberated four days, which in Alabama is enough time to try a capital case and have you ensconced in a berth on Death Row in nearby Atmore. They acquitted Deshaw and another defendant of all charges and all of the defendants of some of the charges. They returned guilty verdicts against Lynn, Eyster and Marshall. Remarkably, the jury found Dickie not guilty of operating a Continuing Criminal Enterprise, the monster felony charge that carried a mandatory life-without-parole sentence and the one that the government had insisted be part of the plea. If the jury's intention had been to temper justice with mercy, it was a pyrrhic gesture. It would be years before Butler's sentences would begin to temper, but at this point it did not matter. The sentencing guidelines were mandatory and the Presentence Report (PSR) piled on all manner of enhancements. He was a manager. He had obstructed justice. There had been all sorts of discussions about guns and talk that had been characterized as death threats. The group's guidelines were high but Dickie's were through the roof. Butler sentenced Eyster to 204 months and Marshall to 293 months. Dickie received seven concurrent life sentences. In two weeks it would be Christmas. It was quite a fall for a man who had it all and Dickie didn't mind telling anyone that he wasn't standing for it. Dickie was whisked away to the penitentiary. Five days into the new year, a guard would call Dickie out of his cell. "Lynn, call your brother. Your mother is dead." Esther Elizabeth Lynn had died of an aneurism.

Chapter 24
A Taste of Honey

On April 23, 1990, the buzz around the Adairsville, Georgia 76 Truck stop was the abandoned mid-sized moving truck that the police had found behind the convenience store. It had been there for days before finally arousing suspicions. Not much happens here in this little city of under 3,000. So, when the police found the vehicle, well, part of it anyway, that was pretty sexy happenings. Probably stolen in nearby Rome or maybe even from Atlanta, everyone figured. But, why leave the cab and chassis of the truck and take the cargo compartment? And, then things really heated up. That hunk of junk was causing all sorts of commotion. Before long there were tons of squad cars and unmarked sedans and all sorts of big city folks buzzing around.

The truck, it was rumored, was linked to someone on the FBI's most wanted list. Two weeks earlier, that three-ton truck had cruised into the Federal Correctional Institution at Talladega, Alabama, ostensibly to deliver vegetables. While it did so, two inmates crawled under the truck and into a trap door that had been built into the cargo area. One of them, Gary Wayne Fowler of Rome, Georgia, was 38 years old and serving a 20-year sentence for a cocaine conviction. He was arrested outside an Atlanta bar only after one month of freedom. The truck, which had been purchased in Birmingham shortly before the jail break, was connected to his family members. It was registered to his dad. His brother Larry, the government claimed, had been the driver. And this wasn't Gary Wayne's first attempt, the police said. He had tried another escape from the jail over in nearby Floyd County a few years before that and the US Marshals Service noted that he had a history of escape and violence for a laundry list of offenses, including kidnaping, hijacking and robbery.

The United States Marshal's Service had, from day one, handled the Lynn prosecution as an extremely-high- security case. Mobile's Marshal had personally written a warning letter to the local jail where they were being detained. He warned them that Lynn and Marshall had "demonstrated strong proclivities for the demonstration of violence." Included in that letter was a DEA-6, a report on each member of the conspiracy that had been arrested. And there was also the matter of their sensitive witnesses like Wood, Jordan, and Pruna and all of the trial hype about threats. Given the sentences that Lynn and the others faced (and, ultimately, received) - and with recent allegations made against Marshall that he was plotting some sort of crazy breakout from the local jail - by sentencing day, security was over-the-top intense. The Bureau of Prisons (BOP) was warned by both the Marshal's Service and the United States Attorney's Office that Lynn and Marshall were escape risks. By the end of the trial, Odom and Dickie had few secrets from each other. Dickie told Odom that he was going to fight his appeal with every ounce of effort that he had but that he was not going to die in prison and would escape if he could. Odom dutifully passed this information along to the Marshals. BOP's instructions to the Marshals were to whisk Lynn and Marshall away from Mobile immediately after sentencing and take them directly to Talladega for safe keeping until an appropriate place could be found. They did, but BOP then dropped the ball. Dickie was not tagged at Talladega as an escape risk or someone who was just there temporarily awaiting a high security assignment. He and Fowler got themselves jobs in the prison kitchen and set out to prove the hand wringers right.

They set out an escape plan. They identified the produce company out of Anniston that supplied the prison. They copied its bill of lading and smuggled it out of the prison. Someone on the outside got an identical vehicle, put company identification on it and constructed a false bulkhead that had been built into the back wall of the truck. On the day of the escape, Fowler's dad called the produce company and, posing as a prison official, told them that the cooler was broken and that the delivery for that day had to be canceled.

Inside the prison, Fowler and Lynn acted on their plan. They were allowed on the loading dock but not if a vehicle was there. The door, secured with nothing more sophisticated than a sliding bolt, was visually inspected by a guard who was seated nearby. Lynn figured out how to manipulate the lock. The truck arrived. The guard went and fetched a pallet jack. Dickie opened the bolt. A piece of cardboard the size of the bolt was taped on the door so as to make it look still secured. They slipped out. They dumped their prison duds in the trash. Their uniforms would soon be hauled away. And just to make sure, they had bribed the trash truck operator. He would not report finding anything unusual. They crawled up into the bulkhead and checked it all out from a peephole. When it finished unloading, the driver went out to the sally port. The cab was searched. The undercarriage was inspected by mirror wands. Even the engine compartment was opened. The truck was clean and free to go.

In Anniston, the two brothers who owned the produce company were having breakfast when one of them mentioned the delivery delay. The brother questioned why, if the prison had 10 coolers, that would be. They contacted the FBI and the FBI contacted the prison. But by then it was too late. Superstar Drug kingpin Dickie Lynn had escaped from an Alabama federal prison in, literally, a turnip truck.

In Dickie's cell the BOP's investigative unit found a note, "10,000 Sunshine." That led them to the driver of the trash truck whose surname was Sunshine. They went to the dump and found the uniforms and presumed that they had somehow gotten out in the compacted trash. It was a puzzlement. How had they not been crushed? But, by then, Dickie had made it to Miami. Eventually, they caught the Fowlers, the son actually wearing a wire on the dad and betraying his brother too. But, Dickie was gone.

U.S. Department of Justice
United States Marshals Service

WANTED
BY U.S. MARSHALS

NOTICE TO ARRESTING AGENCY: Before arrest, validate warrant through National Crime Information Center (NCIC).

United States Marshals Service NCIC entry number: (NIC/ W579214739).

NAME: LYNN, Richard Joseph

ALIAS: DAWBER, Dan; DICKIE, MCCOY, Bob; MILLER, Richard; WEAVER, Tim; LYNN, Dickie

DESCRIPTION:
Sex: ....MALE
Race: ....WHITE
Place of Birth: ....CENTRAL LAKE, MICHIGAN
Date(s) of Birth: ....JULY 19, 1954
Height: ....6'1"
Weight: ....225 LBS
Eyes: ....HAZEL
Hair: ....BROWN
Skintone: ....MEDIUM
Scars, Marks, Tattoos: ....3" SCAR LEFT OUTSIDE FOREARM
Social Security Number: 265-15-7205
NCIC Fingerprint Classification: ..PI 02 13 PO 17 DI 11 10 09 12

SHOULD BE CONSIDERED ARMED AND DANGEROUS
LYNN was serving a life sentence without parole at the time of his escape. LYNN is thought to be in possession of automatic weapons and is a suspect in the contract killing of a drug associate.

WANTED FOR: ESCAPE

Warrant Issued: Northern District of Alabama (Birmingham)
Warrant Number: 9001-0105-A

DATE WARRANT ISSUED: March 27, 1990

MISCELLANEOUS INFORMATION: LYNN was the leader of a large cocaine distribution organization which had direct ties to the Medellin drug cartel operating in Colombia, South America.

If arrested or whereabouts known, notify the local United States Marshals Office, (Telephone: _____).

If no answer, call United States Marshals Service Communications Center in McLean, Virginia.
Telephone (800)336-0102: (24 hour telephone contact) NLETS access code is VAUSMOOOO.
(800)423-0719 (TDD)

Form USM-132
PRIOR EDITIONS ARE OBSOLETE AND NOT TO BE USED
(Rev. 2/84)

Chapter 25
Double Down

On August 29, 1990, things were looking up for John Chapman. The sun was shining, the lunch crowd looked good and on a grander scale, maybe, just maybe, this year the Mississippi legislature would legalize gambling and transform Biloxi from a place with nothing more to offer than tours of Jefferson Davis's home, sleazy bars and ho hum beaches into a major tourist competitor. Chappy's, a flagship Biloxi restaurant, was in full swing, the systemic din a testament to a smooth running machine. Then it threw a rod. Chapman recognized the dysfunctional cacophony. He sensed something was wrong. One of his customers bolted from his lunch, running towards South Nicholson Avenue, away from St. Thomas Catholic Church and up towards Fifth Avenue. He was being chased by armed men. Chapman heard the shots and would later find out that the United States Marshals had captured someone on the FBI's most wanted list right here in his restaurant.

Lynn had been living on the run and had found his way to this sleepy little fishing town. He had left his condo to come have lunch and had been captured in what would later be characterized as "a flurry of gunfire," though the truth be told, it was the task force of federal and local officers who were doing the shooting. Lynn had been high on the FBI's scalp list, but his capture was actually a lucky accident, a gift, a lagniappe. They had been looking for him everywhere: Guatemala, Mexico, Miami, the Keys, but he was in Mississippi, not more than 30 miles from Mobile and was captured as no more than the collateral damage of another project. *Operation Southern Star,* was a nationally- coordinated United States Marshals Service manhunt for fugitives. The program was focused on warrants in major cities. An investigation in Miami had revealed an ongoing drug deal with connections to Mississippi. Lynn just wandered into their crosshairs.

According to Odom, "Dickie's problem was that his money was in Europe and he couldn't get there. So he was trying to get some money together so he could get a passport and get out. He was trying to put together some loads. It was going to be three loads that he was going to bring in to Mississippi. He didn't have a pilot or a plan or anything." Either Dickie or the other fugitive contacted an old source and somewhere down the line they got involved with a Customs snitch and he hooked them up with someone else. They were about to be ripped off by their new partner but they didn't know that. Customs did. They were recording everything. Art Wicks, the Customs Agent who had trailed them in New Orleans, was listening and the more he heard the more he became convinced that it was Dickie. He heard tail numbers mentioned, a crash in Belize, and other mundane details and he connected them to the Lynn case. He became convinced that it was Lynn and called Odom. "I think that's Dickie Lynn."

"I happened to be up in Anniston when they called me and said 'How soon can you get up to Gulfport?'" The next morning, he and Customs Special Agent Charlie Park arrived in Gulfport. "They say, 'You two are the only two that know him on sight so obviously you can't go into the meeting. But we want you out there.' I happen to be in the vehicle at the back of Chappy's Restaurant when it all goes down. Dickie comes flying out the back door and I'm screaming at them to cut him off. 'Cut him off. It's Dickie. It's Dickie.' John Pigott sees Dickie run his hand up under his shirt and cracks a round off in front of him. One of the Customs guys out of New Orleans says 'I fired one round' and I tell him 'You may have but when you pulled the trigger four bullets came out.'"

If life is a constant irony, consider this: two weeks earlier, the Eleventh Circuit - an appellate court with a notoriously conservative record - had overturned the convictions of his two co-defendants Eyster and Marshall, giving them an opportunity to cut a deal with the government. But, because he had absconded, Lynn's appeal was dismissed.

Chapter 26
Andy

The defense team had been surprised when Bedwell rested without calling Pruna. Andy, they knew, was in the building. Bedwell had gone to Miami specifically to debrief him. So, why not use him? "I don't remember why I didn't call him," she responded when asked recently. Bedwell's style is to ring every bell and blow every whistle, to unmercifully pound every piece of evidence over a defendant's head, especially when she has a superstar witness and a superstar case. Maybe she figured that it was enough that Pruna's role had been established through her direct and by the defense's cross-examination. Andy's connection to the Alabama loads and the Columbian dope was firmly established. "We didn't do anything without checking with Andy, getting Andy's okay," Purvis had said. "The night of the airplane crash, we went directly to a phone and notified him. I would say that Andy Prunas, (sic) nothing would have happened without him. I mean he was the man when you got down to the last guy in charge, that was Andy Prunas."

It certainly wasn't lost on her, especially considering the sport that they had with Wood, that Pruna had some heavy baggage and that it might be more hurtful than good to present such a target. Pruna, Black had foreshadowed during his opening, was "a very clever fellow." So clever that he had even managed to scam the government. He had been a fugitive when the feds arrested his brother Fernando and held him without bail. Andy worked out a deal with the government, Black told the jury, "release my brother on bail and I will surrender." But he reneged and both of them became fugitives. Fernando fled to Argentina and Andy went underground. At his subsequent arrest, Andy - now faced with yet another indictment - was found in possession of some heavy armaments - seven weapons, including an AR-15 - and a false Venezuelan passport with authentic certification. There were also allegations about one of their couriers, a

Pruna relative, who had wound up dead in the Everglades, his motor home set afire and 200 keys missing, everyone in the group pointing fingers at each other. Bedwell could be sure that Black and Bronis were prepared for Pruna.

But the fact that Bedwell did not use Pruna was due most probably to things beyond this case. Both Prunas maintained connections to the Cuban underground. While Kennedy's "disposal problem" was probably really more about a political hot potato than a Trojan Horse, the CIA's warnings about what happens to such men - men who have outlived their short term usefulness - was prophetic. "You train them and put them in business, it's not that easy to turn them off," Kennedy had been told. While his brother was rotting in a Cuban jail, Andy had followed other members of *Brigada 2506* and had gotten a Navy commission and worked with the Naval Research Laboratory. But, like many of the Bay of Pigs invaders, he wound up in drug trafficking.

Perhaps more. The Cuban underground was the proverbial genie out of the bottle, wreaking vengeance on Castro, communism, and, some say, maybe even on Kennedy himself. Presidents Kennedy and Johnson were succeeded by Nixon. What had started hot on the heels of the Bay of Pigs fiasco with *Operation Mongoose*, developed into a dirty little laundry list of sordid Latin American intrigues that bore this country's fingerprints. Cuban expatriates often served as proxy mercenaries. By 1989, the list included *Operation Condor,* Argentina's Dirty Little War, Iran-Contra, the overthrow of Bolivia and Chile, political assassinations and more. Some of these players had even been involved in domestic intrigues like Watergate and the assassination of the Chilean General Orlando Leerier in Washington, D.C. When Fernando needed refuge, Andy had connections in Argentina where he had been a military advisor during its "Dirty Little War."

Prior to the beginning of the trial, Black had filed a "brush back" motion pursuant to the Classified Information Procedures Act giving notice that he would elicit testimony about classified information. Asked about the basis for his motion, Black pointed to "substantial things in Mr. Pruna's background regarding intelligence agencies and regarding this case." Deshaw's attorney had mentioned that the defendants had been involved in the Iran-Contra arms scandal. The docket sheets reveal filings of confidential information by Schmidgall. Lynn's subsequent habeas filing would make allegations concerning the Prunas and Jordan and their connection to intelligence activities that had resulted in the Boland Amendment, legislation aimed at restricting assistance to the Contras in Nicaragua.

Odom gives substance to this. "Nobody from the CIA had a conversation with me. I doubt that they had a conversation with Gloria, but they influenced the situation to the point that we were basically told that if Andy Pruna takes the stand, he is not going to answer any questions because of what the defense is going to know and what they can bring out in this trial. It's going to be...it would be of a national security interests and we're not going to get into that. He's going to invoke national security and is not going to answer any questions."

Celestino Mendez, the man whose pivotal testimony had been the proverbial nail in the horse's shoe, the man that had caused the fall of, at the very least, three drug empires, the defendant on whose behalf an Assistant United States Attorney had traveled to Maine, was sentenced to twenty years. Andy Pruna? He fared much better. Despite not having had to testify and having committed all sorts of mischief for the government, Pruna was sentenced to 12 years, his time to run concurrently on the three federal prosecutions he faced in Alabama and Florida.

Two years later, Fernando Pruna, who with the assistance of his brother had been a fugitive from justice, was sentenced to 12 years to run concurrently with charges in all of his indictments. Andy's sentence was then further reduced to 10 years upon the government's subsequent motion for reduction of sentence. On December 29, 1994 he was released from custody after having served about 3½ years. Eighteen months after Andy's release, the government filed a motion for reduction of sentence on behalf of Fernando Pruna. He was released from federal custody the next day. He had served 3½ years.

Chapter 27
Charlie Jordan

Lynn's claim to having an inside man at Customs was no mere braggadocio. Their "inside man" even had his own crew of inside men. Lynn didn't have a mere agency employee. He had one of the chiefs. Charles Jordan was a Customs Supervisor in charge of the all-important Upper Keys office at Key Largo. Bedwell had him prepped and ready to go. It had been Jordan who introduced Dickie to Pruna. Like Pruna, Jordan had some major baggage. Jordan was the rotten apple that threatened to despoil the counter-narcotics mechanism. The recurring allegations that federal agents were on the take had been percolating within the three major law enforcement agencies and had spawned multiple internal investigations that would eventually focus on him. "Employees who sell their badges and the trust of their fellow workers are committing treason against the United States and should be punished as traitors to their country and the United States Customs Service," an outraged agency official proclaimed. Criminal prosecutions were initiated in California, Louisiana, and Florida.

The first indictment issued in 1985 in New Orleans. It accused Jordan and three other Customs agents of assisting in the importation of about 52,000 pounds of marijuana and of providing the traffickers with sensitive information from Custom's computers. Although the other agents were convicted, Jordan walked. Having caught lightning in the bottle once, though, he apparently thought it prudent to abscond. That left William Wallace, Jr. holding the bag for the 1987 trial in Miami. Based at Homestead Air Force Base near Miami, Wallace had been in charge of the Customs intercept pilots. He and Jordan were accused of helping to import cocaine by steering the Customs patrol boats away from the drop zones. They were also charged with attempting to import cocaine in 1983 and 610 pounds of marijuana in 1984 from Plana City, Bahamas, to Marco Island off the southwest coast of Florida in an amphibious aircraft that Wallace had purchased.

Jordan was also accused of bringing in 5,000 pounds of marijuana from Jamaica to the Keys. "They did it without any fear of law enforcement, without any fear of Custom boats and planes," Assistant United States Attorney Myles H. Malman said. "When there's $1.5 million at stake, there's going to be, unfortunately, corruption." The following year, with Wood's debriefing under their belt, a Miami grand jury issued yet another drug smuggling indictment for Jordan, this time linking him, Wallace and two more Customs officials with the Prunas and accusing them of smuggling nearly 40 tons of cocaine and marijuana into the country.

The government finally caught Jordan in 1989. He had been the focus of a massive and bizarre manhunt spanning more than three years. The fox in the hen house, he had become grist for the crime show mill and had been featured on cop shows like *America's Most Wanted*. His odyssey finally ended on a summer day in 1989 at a Wyoming trailer park near Yellowstone National Park. A stranded motorist requested his assistance starting his car because his battery was dead. But no good deed goes unpunished. The Good Samaritan was soon confronted with the motorist's startling assertion. He had a machine gun taped to his arms, he told Jordan. If he didn't do exactly as the stranger instructed, he would be "cut in half." The "motorist" was John William Juhasz, a federal agent who had doggedly been on Jordan's trail. Jordan and his wife Delores were taken into custody.

Maybe it was his baggage. Maybe, again, she thought the trial had dragged on long enough. Most probably it was whatever information Jordan was giving up. But, even though he had been prepped and announced as a witness, Bedwell didn't call Jordan either. She didn't have to, really. The federal rules allow "co-conspirator statements." She got his story to the jury through Wood. "Charlie Jordan owned or lived in a home right around the corner from where Ricou Deshaw's parents lived," he told them. "And apparently Mr. Jordan was approaching Ricou, something about some kind of common working agreement. He wanted to work for Ricou and which essentially at that time Ricou was essentially working for me. So he came to me and said 'Do you want to use this guy? He could provide us information.' And at that time I wasn't interested. At that point, we were scared of him. Ricou was himself. And I think Charlie tried to prove his worth when he showed him the report from Meridian, Mississippi. At some point thereafter, they went into an active working agreement or that is what they told me."

"First of all, Charlie wanted to sell us advance information on the Customs surveillance, which we didn't purchase. Or at least I never did," Wood told the jury. "And the next thing I know, like I say, he switched his plane and switched his operation to New Orleans. And they told me that Charlie introduced him to a Customs agent in New Orleans who was, to quote Mr. Deshaw, giving them approach instructions in New Orleans when they would fly the loads of marijuana in they would go right over the guy's house supposedly. That led him to, in November of '85, on Thanksgiving day of 1985, Charlie Jordan arranged some kind of a deal with those guys to air drop some cocaine to the back country of the Florida Keys."

According to Dickie, "We were caught almost before we started. Ricou and I went up to Louisiana. We used to race boats. We met one of the drivers. He told us about his catfish farm up in Opelousas that has canals that we could drop loads into and we went up there to look at it." The guy was being followed. Some kids broke into a barn where he had stored some pot. They got caught and snitched. The sheriff started an investigation and set up a wiretap. "Me and Ricou flew up there right in the middle of it. I called him up and said 'I'm over here at the airport.'" They flew up to the farm and charted out potential landing strips, flew back and dropped him off and continued on to Meridian to go turkey hunting.

Customs was on their trail. They were followed to Baton Rouge where the agents unsuccessfully tried to break into the airplane and put a transponder on it. They were followed to Meridian where the agents reported that they had offloaded duffle bags probably containing contraband, not knowing it was just hunting gear. But the damage was done. They were now on the radar. And they would even know it. When Lynn went to return the van, the rental agent showed him a business card. "This guy came by asking a lot of questions about you." Lynn looked at the card. It said "United States Customs Special Agent Arthur Wicks, New Orleans, Louisiana."

When they returned from their hunting trip they were accosted by Jordan who asked Deshaw what the hell he was doing in Louisiana. "We didn't know Charlie was corrupt," Dickie said. "He threw the reports on the table and said 'Read those.' Ricou read them and he said 'When you want to do something in Louisiana, you need to get with me because all my guys that I trained are up there as agents. Any time you want to do something, just holler.' We had no idea because he was the head guy down there. He was the head of South Florida."

They came to trust him completely when Jordan called Dickie and told him something only Lynn would know. "Your plane is sitting in Naples Airport, isn't it?" The plane was being used to smuggle marijuana through Louisiana, was now on Customs' radar and a judge had authorized a tracking device on the plane, he told Dickie. "They put a transponder on it when the plane landed in Pell City. Meet me there at midnight and I'll show you where it is." And that is how Lynn met Pruna. "Charlie says, 'I have this guy and he wants to airdrop cocaine back in the bay.' We started working with Andy."

Some time later, the Jordan case would resurrect itself into the national spotlight, this time centered around the issue of whether his capture was plain vanilla cop work or some other exotic-flavored concoction. Jordan had become such a high profile fugitive that the government spared no energy in desperately trying to locate him, his case conveniently dovetailing with the government's flirtation with the paranormal. *Stargate*, a secret project borne of the Cold War and the fear that the Soviets might spring an ESP *Manhattan Project* on us, was the newest incantation of governmental experiments in psychic phenomena policing. Using something called "remote viewing," they would attempt to locate hostages, divine secrets and locate crashed airplanes.

The Jordan case came at an opportune time for *Stargate*. Its original manifestation had been funded by the CIA and concentrated on matters of national security. An teat on a governmental udder that was running dry, *Stargate's* results were increasingly being questioned. Future funding looked bleak. Then they realized what everyone knows, that there's a lot of money to be made from drugs. Because it involves our national boundaries, drug smuggling necessarily blurs the lines of the Posse Comitatus Act, the law that says that the military can't be involved in civilian law enforcement. *Stargate* erased them.

There had been a move to unify command and control of drug interdiction that began with President Clinton and culminated in the National Defense Authorization Act. The Department of Defense was charged with the detection, monitoring, and interdiction of aerial and maritime traffic. The country was divided into Joint Task Forces. One of them was headquartered in the Keys. *Stargate* now had a new *raison d'etre*, finding bad guys here and they had a new deep pocket. Five months after being tasked with finding him, he was under arrest, beginning the debate about how his capture occurred.

On May 26, 1995, Charles Jordan, the Customs supervisor that had been the focus of an investigation into monumental governmental corruption, who had absconded and had been the subject of a major man hunt - and who, again, had not testified - was released from federal custody after doing very little jail time.

Chapter 28
Ricou Redux

Rugged sportsman, pilot, and ex-football player Ricou Deshaw cried and literally fell out when the not guilty verdict was announced. He kissed the ground. The jury, who had not been privy to Odom's assessment, agreed. Ricou "hadn't done shit" in the Southern District or, if he had, he had abandoned the conspiracy. And he hadn't even taken the stand. Or had he? Bedwell's direct examination of Kevin Sheehy appeared to limit Ricou's prior involvement with Dickie to one marijuana load in 1984 and that was in Florida. Steve Purvis testified that Ricou had not been involved in the initial Wood load, had been involved in a couple of the grass field loads but had left well before they switched to Demopolis. It was Wood who claimed he had been there. Tony Chambless, who had almost immediately begun making secret recordings of conversations with Deshaw, Purvis and Turpin, came across as the most grounded, likeable and pitiable of the witnesses. He had been a reluctant participant, a local without any prior background in anything but blue-collar work, a seeker of thrills in nothing more exotic than turkey hunting. He had gotten out immediately and, just as immediately, naively confessed. And, if that wasn't enough to show his contrition, here he was playing secret agent man when it was obvious that his typecasting was more *Dukes of Hazard* than James Bond. So he had to be handled with kid gloves, something Lazzara would have to confront as this was the main "clean" witness against Deshaw.

Not that bluster was Lazzara's style. His style, laid back and almost self-effacing, was perfect for a witness that came across as humble and contrite. Nor would he have gotten away with picking on a witness. One of the rationales for the restrictive nature of federal prosecutions is that it limits the amount of extraneous information a lawyer can get into a case.

"Speaking objections" are less likely in a federal trial. Testifying witnesses - their personal space protected on the stand by a buffer, a no-man's land through which a lawyer must ask permission to enter - are in an even larger protective bubble when it comes to cross-examination. Anything even close to a heated exchange is subject to being found "argumentative." But a smart lawyer uses what is out there and that is what Lazzara did with his cross-examination of Chambless and his utilization of the undercover tapes.

What Lazzara had was those tapes - the tapes introduced by the government and not by the defense. They allowed Ricou to testify without taking the stand and being grilled by Bedwell. Chambless had made twelve undercover recordings of his conversations with Deshaw and they contained a host of exculpatory and self-serving statements, some pretty harsh commentary on governmental tactics, as well as a laundry list of mundane but somewhat salient personal details.

Lazzara got Chambless to pinpoint the times he had actually seen Deshaw in Alabama and was able to limit Deshaw's exposure to many of the counts by establishing that Ricou had been elsewhere or that, by that time, there had been a falling out with Dickie. The tapes contained Deshaw's assertions that he had not been present on the night of the Hartley crash, that he had been in flight school, etc. Even if the jury believed Chambless' testimony that Ricou had been involved in one or two of the earliest loads, they were remote and unique. Lazzara had by now humanized Deshaw and put before the jury the tremendous penalties and human drama at stake and a litany of other concerns, like the fact that he had young children, a war hero brother and commercial airline pilot dad, his concern for his wife's safety, etc.

Lazzara established that Chambless, too, had essentially withdrawn from the conspiracy but that he still maintained ties with the hunting camp. The first time he met Deshaw, Chambless told the jury, was when Ricou brought some of his professional football player friends to the camp. It was the first of many hunting trips made by Deshaw, sometimes accompanied by his family, sometimes with his friends. Chambless recounted them all and admitted that they had nothing to do with drugs.

But, most importantly, Lazzara got Chambless to agree that Deshaw had withdrawn from the conspiracy. "Now, you know that Mr. Deshaw ceased his participation with that camp, don't you?" "Yes sir." "Long before you did, isn't that correct?" "After that...after March of '86 when they brought the load of drugs and, at the latter part of turkey season, Ricou came up and had his family with him and his friends, like we discussed a few minutes ago, and that is when he called me off to the side out there, just me and him by himself and told me that some helicopters had flew over while they was down there at the strip that night and scared him real bad and he had thought a lot about it and decided he was through with all of that and that he wanted me to know it, he wanted me to know he was through with it."

"And that ended his association with the camp, as far you were concerned?" "Yes." "Sometime around turkey season?" "Yes sir.""And you said, I think, on direct examination, that Ricou asked you to help him to get the other people to cut that out, cut out their activity, do you remember that?" "Ricou, when he called me off to the side, he said 'It is going to keep happening until we convince Dickie to quit doing it. It's going to get a lot of people in trouble around here.' And he said 'We need to', you know, 'stick together and tell Dickie that they're watching that strip down there,' that the strip was being watched.'"

"Do you remember Ricou telling you," Lazzara asked, "'I walked away from these people four years ago and they are still coming, they are still coming at me?'" He underscored the point that Ricou had told him that he was "scared to death because they were telling him he was looking at life imprisonment."

Lazzara had gotten Purvis and Howard Carrell, Woody's brother-in-law, to contradict Chambless' assertion that Deshaw had been present when Woody came up to inspect the camp. Then, he got Chambless to refute most of Wood's testimony concerning that same incident and he did it with surgical precision and comedic effect. "Was he in that plane with y'all that day y'all flew around to look at that strip?" "No sir." "Are you sure?" "I am positive." Lazzara pushed the point. "If Wood claimed to have been in the plane he would be mistaken." "If he was in the plane I would be mistaken." "Somebody would be mistaken, either you or him if he was in the plane?" "As far as I know Wood wasn't in the plane unless he was up under the seat." The jury laughed.

Lazzara had also been hugely successful in eliciting a lot of self-serving statements about Ricou's lack of culpability and Wood's utter malfeasance through Kevin Sheehy. Wood's testimony about Ricou, according to Kevin, was largely fabricated. Ricou was not present, Sheehy said, on the night of the crash. "That's a fact." Ricou had sold his interest in the camp a long time before that, Sheehy explained and had withdrawn from all of the activities. And, although Ricou had known about the impending charges, he had been determined to fight them and had refused to run. Kevin testified that Ricou had told him that he was afraid Wood was going to tell lies about him and that he was "afraid the government might pressure other people to tell lies on him." Ricou had told him that he "didn't want to run from anything he hadn't done."

Ricou was acquitted of all charges. His problems, however, were far from over. A grand jury in the Eastern District of Louisiana had returned an eleven-count indictment against him, Lynn, Bagalman and others for their marijuana boat drops. Because the Mobile case had been a CCE and encompassed the conduct in the other indictments, he filed a partially successful appeal on Double Jeopardy grounds. He still, however, had a remaining RICO (Racketeer Influenced and Corrupt Organization) charge in Louisiana, two indictments in the Northern District of Alabama and another in Miami. He engaged in a five-year appeals battle and when it ran its unsuccessful course, he cut a deal. Ricou pled to two different indictments and received a 14-year sentence.

Chapter 29
Holding The Bag

American jurisprudence is supposedly based on the principle that it is better for a guilty man to go free than that an innocent man go to prison, a rationale that originally formed the basis of many of the rules in our criminal system. We also championed the semblance of parity between the accused and accuser. But, more and more, those notions have become weakened and seen as just "pretty" ideals that can't always be met. We have almost completely retreated from the idea that the individual must be protected from the power and overreach of the government. The prophylactic rules designed to keep that power in check have been bent, hammered, and almost eviscerated beyond recognition.

    The Bail Reform Act of 1984 did not just hasten the erosion of parity. It created a chasm, an Orwellian nightmare for persons accused that fundamentally changed the criminal justice system. The basic presumption that one is entitled to bail was reversed and became "rebuttable" in drug prosecutions. While there was the initial resistance to this notion, today, we've almost abandoned the idea that bail is a right. Pre-trial detention is the norm in federal drug cases. The act established a carrot-and-stick approach to sentencing. A tiny carrot at that. The Federal Sentencing guidelines is a points system for grading defendants. Congress' warped vision of justice was that there was too much "disparity" in sentencing and that it needed to be "equalized." Like Jung's example of the "ideal average," the effect is that this abstract mean treats people as if they are nothing more than fungible, no more complex than lima beans that need grading.

    A defendant is plugged into little taxonomic categories that are dependent on, primarily, criminal history and the quantity of drugs. These two categories form the axes which, along with other factors, comprise a sentencing point system. This quest for "uniformity" and "parity" is an artifice. It has redefined the parameters of the process by adding structure and process but it is just as subjective. The United States Probation Office is a greater part of the mix. The probation officer, the judge and the prosecution are now a governmental sentencing *menage a trois*. A Presentence Report Investigation (PSR) is prepared that calculates sentencing guidelines. Points are added or subtracted for things like "acceptance of responsibility," leadership roles, etc., and often what goes into those calculations depends on how cozy the defendant has become with the government or how much of a hammer it is perceived needs to come down on an uncooperative defendant.

The stick is "determinate sentencing," a cudgel of increased sentences and the amount of time actually served. Thanks to these changes this country is now on par with just about every totalitarian country for its rates of imprisonment and range of punishments. What used to be disparagingly called a "trial tax," an increased jail term for putting the prosecution to the task of trial, is no longer something that happens *sub rosa*; it has been codified as an official sentencing sanction. If a defendant has the temerity to actually demand a trial, he or she will be punished upon conviction. If the defendant testifies his or her guidelines will increase for "obstruction of justice," concurrently losing the "acceptance of responsibility" points given to those who plead early. A judge may even use acquitted conduct in determining "relevant conduct." The Act also further reduced any semblance of parity between the parties by giving the government a monopoly on the ability to make a reduction-of-sentence motion. Neither the defendant nor the judge can move to reduce a sentence, only the prosecutor.

In most state courts, the plea bargaining process is pretty straight forward. A defendant reaches an agreement with the prosecution. If it is rejected by the court, the guilty plea can be withdrawn. Not so in federal court. It is the rare case that is allowed under the rule that allows a defendant to withdraw his or her plea. And a defendant must enter into a plea - a plea that cannot subsequently be withdrawn - without knowing more than the bare bones of what a sentence will be. The guidelines are formulated much later by a probation officer. Federal plea agreements are onerous one-way contracts that routinely contain waivers of appeal rights and put the prosecutor firmly in command. There are other things - like mandatory minimums, expansion of the definition of hearsay and the use of "collateral evidence" (but, not so, if the defendant attempts to use it) - that a defendant encounters as a fork in the road; jump from a who-knows-how-high cliff or engage in a pyrrhic David and Goliath battle.

But there still remain some arguments in the criminal defense lawyer's bag of rocks. One of those is outrageous governmental misconduct or prosecutorial misconduct and one of the seminal cases is *United States v. Eyster* where Bedwell is portrayed as the villain. Now mind you, it's one thing to have a defense, another to make it work, especially in federal court, and certainly in the Eleventh Circuit. Successful prosecutorial misconduct complainants, like those claiming entrapment or ineffective assistance of counsel, are about as successful as Sisyphus. It is difficult to shock the conscience of a federal judge. It is even more so when three of them have to reach the consensus that the government has done something wrong.

So, what did Bedwell supposedly do? People who question how it is that a criminal defense lawyer does this type of work not only ignore the grand notions we have about the protection of the accused, they just don't understand the real world part of criminal law. It's not necessarily the job of either side to have a straight up or down win. A "loss" or a "win" depends on an accurate evaluation of the case and the result one gets; the best result is a just one. There are five sides to the equation in a criminal prosecution and if a case goes to trial it's because, for whatever reason, someone made that case go to trial. It can be pinned on the judge, the client, or the two opposing lawyers.

It is the trial lawyer who is truly sensitive to the reality; no matter how good or bad a case is, there's no telling what a jury will do. If the case "goes bad" it won't be the judge who rejected the plea bargain as "too lenient" or the defendant who insisted on an apology from the President who will be blamed. It will fall on the head of the prosecutor who lost the "lock" case or the defense lawyer who "skinned up" his or her client. It is this prospect that grounds both lawyers, although sometimes it is conflicting egos or politics that have made them cross their Rubicon and come here for full-scale war.

The five-week trial had plenty of colorable appellate fodder - the constant introduction of the Defendants' supposed propensity for violence, guns, explosives, the plethora of "prior bad acts" that dated back years and involved other substances, etc. But, that this federal conviction was in fact reversed involved the confluence of many factors peculiar to this case and some sort of unexplained and cosmic disturbance in Atlanta where the Eleventh Circuit is based. It was due mostly, though, to the amazing amalgam of great lawyers whose skill and tenacity eventually carried the day. They understood that the beginning of a trial is only the continuation of a longitudinal process and that the game is never over. All of the defense lawyers had made numerous pretrial objections. They may have lost those motions but they never lost sight of the end game, the appeal. Throughout the trial they used witness testimony not only to infect the government's case with reasonable doubt but to mine it for things which substantiated the bases for their pre-trial objections. It would be their cross-examination of witnesses that would lead the appellate court to discount much of the trial testimony.

In presenting Sheehy, Bedwell did as she had done with the testimony of Purvis, Deweese, Wood, and the others; she elicited his testimony about every impeachable negative that he had. This is a basic trial skill and is designed to minimize issues that can be exploited by the opposing side. She got him to testify about his priors, that he had pled guilty and that he had a deal with the government. And, just as they had done with Purvis, Deweese, Wood and the others, they started picking Kevin apart, hoping, as a criminal defense lawyer sees it, to "make chicken salad out of chicken shit." They did and it was Sheehy's testimony about an unimportant detail upon which they seized.

Black began by walking Sheehy back through what he had just said and putting it on the blackboard. Yes, Sheehy conceded, he had been in jail during the commission of the acts that formed the basis of Count 7. Kevin explained that he had only become involved on the night of the crash, Count 9 of the indictment. Sheehy, however, had pled guilty to Count 7. "Are you telling us that you pled guilty to something that you're innocent of?" Black asked, a cut so deft its damage went unnoticed.

Bronis turned up the heat. Sheehy conceded the obvious: that he had told his lawyer that he had not been there for the Count 7 activities; had pled only four days before the trial; had taken an oath and entered a plea; that he had been asked by the judge whether he was pleading guilty because he was, in fact, guilty; and that Sheehy had responded 'Yes, sir, I am pleading guilty because I am guilty.' Bronis, whose sense of outrage is apparently boundless, jumped him. "And that was a lie?" Kevin's response that it was only "technically speaking" a lie appeared anticipated by Bronis. He had Sheehy firmly in his grip. "There's no technically about it. That was a lie, point blank, to this judge four days before this trial began, was it not?" Kevin was now putty in Bronis' hands. He conceded it was a lie and would have probably conceded to just about anything else that was suggested. "But in order to get the benefit of this deal, you felt it was in your best interests to lie four days before this trial began, correct?" "Yes."

That might have ended it had Bedwell not responded in kind and a cat fight not ensued. It began with her attempt to rehabilitate Sheehy and when, according to Bronis, she "waltzed over" to the board. She showed Sheehy the indictment, correctly pointing out that Count 9 involved the crash at Demopolis. But she went further. At the board she physically changed Black's notation. "So if this seven was actually a nine, it would be a reference to the instance when you were, is that right?" Lazzara was uncharacteristically apoplectic. Black jumped in, saying sarcastically that "If a pig was a cow we could get milk out of it." Butler, usually nonplussed and quick to smooth over anything that might be perceived as trial error, angrily dressed Black down for his impertinence, overruled the defense objections and allowed Bedwell to proceed but she was just shooting more holes in the bottom of the boat.

Bedwell's weak spot is that she is thin-skinned and considers herself a righteous messenger of good. So when Bronis accused her of making bad faith arguments she took it beyond the professional. She launched into possible explanations but was at this point, like Ginger Rogers, improvising under Bronis' strong lead. She continued making the point with Sheehy that it was merely a typographical error of no importance. She offered other possible reasons for the mistake. She asked Sheehy whether Sessions had been present when his plea was taken. Sessions had negotiated most of the pleas himself so this was obviously true. According to Sheehy's lawyer, Sessions was definitely there. He remembers that day very well, he says, because it was so hectic and part of the docket included the Lynn case which, of course, meant an extra security presence and a carnival buzz in the air. "Jeff was overseeing everything. I'm thinking there were 200 people in Judge Hand's courtroom, maybe 250. There were all sorts of out-of-town lawyers there and tons of defendants. It was a status call and people were changing their pleas and they were taking guilty pleas. It was a circus. My personal opinion is that she just made a mistake."

But Bronis saw it as obfuscation and he wouldn't back down, even from Butler's stern hand. He was like a pit bull clamping down on to what he indignantly characterized as a capital infraction by Bedwell. He attacked her and asked for proof, again with no quarter given. Butler slapped him down hard. Butler denied the defense lawyers' subsequent motions for a new trial and they were denied. Bronis still would not stop.

He submitted a transcript that questioned Sessions' presence. He never stopped pressing. He confronted every apologia as a fabrication. He did not stop even after the closing of the government's case, at sentencing and, having now made a hell of a record, on appeal. The point that would forever remain unclear had been underscored and exacerbated and would form the basis for the appellate court's opinion. Sessions and Bedwell might have taken the plea together. He may have walked out leaving her to finish or it may have been only Gloria. It didn't matter. It became an important issue and an unimportant explanation.

And Bronis won. In the end, Bedwell, who had not been part of the plea negotiations, had belatedly taken on the job single-handedly because her boss didn't want to share the credit with another district, and who had been given what turned out to be only an empty promise of assistance, went down on her sword. It looked like she had implied facts that were, at best, not in evidence. Whether she made an honest mistake or she was right and it was someone else's fault didn't matter, she represented the government and now stood accused of having used its prestige to improperly vouch for the credibility of a witness, thus tarnishing the integrity of the judicial process.

Anyone who does federal defender appellate work knows that reversals are usually won by the government and have learned to fear the phrase "No harmless error." It usually comes at the end of a long list of enumerated trial errors that the court recognizes have happened, but that it somehow rationalizes as unimportant, *de minimis* in court-speak, just not enough to overturn a conviction.

They won. The court zeroed in on the credibility of the plea-bargained witnesses. "The closing arguments of the prosecutor and the defendants principally involved the credibility of these witnesses and the nature and extent of the corroborating evidence." It parsed out the testimony remarkably well, especially considering the number of counts upon which a "no harm, no foul" decision could have been relied upon.

They not only set out the laundry list of testimonial inconsistencies and contradictions, they actually compared the testimony to the counts of acquittal as proof that the government's witnesses had not been believed by the jury.

From day one, Odom had disagreed with giving Abbott and Clark total immunity, partly because he questioned their veracity. It didn't make sense, he argued, that Hartley had been paid $300,000 and that Clark had gotten so much less. "Those two assholes are lying through their teeth," he had told Corum. "They're lying about stuff they don't want us to know about like how much money they got. That son of a bitch says that Abbott got $50,000 for co-piloting. I wasn't born yesterday. They got more money than that." Odom also questioned the deal with Wood, again, for the reason that it defied logic and that it was allowing Wood's unjust enrichment. Both of those, however, had been out of his hands.

Not so for the appellate court. It seized on the issue of the monies paid to the pilots, finding Clark and Abbott's assertions as not inconsequential lies. Their utter lack of credibility had not been lost on the jury, the appellate court opined, noting that "Clark and Abbott had complete immunity in exchange for their testimony despite earning between $700,000 and $1 million for their smuggling." Clark had every reason in the world to avoid capture. As a two-time loser facing the new drug guidelines, he would do an eternity in prison. But that he would lie when he had such a great deal showed just what a miscreant he remained and the trial record proved it.

While Bronis' approach was to flay witnesses and beat them into submission, Black's *modus operandi* was subtlety, the death of a thousand paper cuts. He gently peeled away the lies as if they were the petals of an onion. In his cross-examination of Clark, he started with the seemingly inconsequential and worked his way to the core. There had been a hint of romance to Clark's Vaiden Field getaway. Black dispelled any illusion that it was anything but a maniacal act. Purvis had testified that Clark had

turned on all of the plane's lights and had headed straight for the police cars in a desperate game of chicken. "I believe that if they hadn't gotten out of his way they would have rammed each other."
Black got the mechanical details from Clark. The plane's nose would come up when it reached a ground speed of 65 miles-per-hour and lift off at 70, Clark told Black. It would take 600 or 700 feet to reach that speed. Where, Black asked, were the police cars at the time the wheels left the ground. "I was on the west side of the strip. They were on the east side of the strip. One had headed towards me and I turned the nose gear which is the steerable leg toward himself and he went to the left and I went back to the right. I was approximately, to get to that, 100 feet." How fast were the police cars going? "I don't know. It was at night."

Black pressed. "It would have made quite a crash though if you had hit the police cars?" Clark tried an evasive maneuver. "That was never a consideration." But Clark is now in a courtroom, not a plane. Black kept coming. "My question though, it would have made quite a crash if you had hit the police cars, wouldn't it?" Clark finally answered that "Oh, yes," it would have. Impact. Clark's escapade was now in its true context. But for good fortune, he and Abbott and the officers on the ground could easily have wound up like the Hartleys. But, more importantly, it showed that Clark would do anything to keep from getting caught.

Clark knew how to play the system and Black set out to show that. Clark had previously been indicted in another district. Black pointed out how Clark had made a plea bargain and had pleaded for mercy by representing himself as a poor unfortunate who had merely been the victim of an impetuous mistake and yet, here he was again, getting a second bite of the apple.

Clark acknowledged the Faustian nature of his current plea agreement. He had agreed to assist in locating any assets, surrender cash or substantial assets for forfeiture, be truthful and honest and not withhold any materials. Failure to comply with the conditions of the agreement made it null and void and subjected him to the full prosecution for all the crimes he had committed and allowed the government, he agreed, to ask for the maximum punishment in the highest possible custodial level in prison.

His house had been protected from forfeiture due to his representation that it had not been purchased with drug proceeds. Black showed the utter impossibility that it was free from taint. Cornered, Clark was forced to admit that the statement was false. Black also established that he had lied to the agents about how much money he had made, that he and Abbott had concocted a story, that he was fully aware of the consequences of lying, and that nothing had happened to him as a result. Clark twisted in the breeze interminably as Black hit him with his lies and inconsistencies, things that the government had accepted at face value and that were only now being revealed.

He made a million dollars. Where did it go? Pressed for an answer, he claimed that he kept it "around the house" and still had $275,000 left. Black asked sardonically, "In a sock drawer?" He hadn't told the agents or prosecutors that he had the cash. "I was never asked. I didn't tell them. Right now I told them." The government had hidden him and he had hidden the money nearby, he said. "I bought a five gallon paint container with a top that snaps on it and it is in two of those."

In parsing out the testimony the appellate court noted that Clark had testified that "Bobby" operated the radios in Alabama. He even met this "Bobby" in Tampa. "But Clark never identified Eyster as someone he spoke with on the radio and was unable to identify a photograph of Eyster as this 'Bobby,'" it reasoned. Abbott, who could not identify Eyster as someone he spoke with during his flights, did claim that Lynn had told him that Eyster operated the radios for the Vaiden Field load. But, the court noted, the jury acquitted Eyster on the counts relating to this incident. Both of them had linked Marshall with the Demopolis incident but neither witness offered evidence concerning Eyster and Marshall during the period they cooperated with the government. They continued, discounting the testimony of every one of the government's witnesses. Purvis was a consistent drug user. Deweese, on parole, gave apparent inconsistent statements under oath, as had Barclay.

Sheehy's, it turns out, was pivotal testimony. Sheehy had claimed to have helped Eyster set up the radios. He had overheard conversations between Lynn and the pilots. After the crash he had gone to New Orleans with them. He placed Marshall in Alabama during several loads and had Marshall driving product to Florida. "No physical evidence was introduced connecting Eyster to the drug trafficking organization and his conviction rested heavily on Sheehy's testimony," the court said. "Purvis, Deweese, and Barclay all linked Eyster to numerous importations that formed the basis of the several substantive counts against Eyster. The jury, however, acquitted Eyster on all counts with the exception of Count 9."

The analysis was simple, if somewhat amazing for a usually skeptical appellate court. The jury acquitted Eyster on all counts, with the exception of Count 9, the count Sheehy testified about and which had caused the uproar. Apparently, then, the jury credited only Sheehy's testimony and rejected Purvis, Deweese, and Barclay's, making Bedwell's comments "an unfair and foul blow."

Chapter 30
Mercy?

Does Lynn deserve a break? Leave aside for the moment the philosophical argument that federal sentences, especially in drug cases, are not rational punishments, that they are over-the-top and designed to extort information and assist in prosecutions. The best argument is that the trial was critically flawed. Lynn's appeal was dismissed despite the fact that the Eleventh Circuit overturned the other convictions because it was an unfair trial. But because of a technicality, a life sentence of imprisonment stands. It is a miscarriage of justice.

The Eleventh Circuit recognized that the jury had discounted much of the testimony. But, neither the jury nor the appellate court could know what would ultimately be revealed about Davenport's credibility. And it was Davenport and Wardle that had painted the sinister picture of guns and claymore mines and even talk of executions. Jack Marshall is the third victim in this comic opera. A biker who looked the part, he was painted as a knuckle-dragging thug and the group's enforcer. He presented a palpable presence to the Lurp fantasies painted by Wardle and Davenport. And because he was framed as the nefarious part of the plot, his punishment was the next longest, even though he had probably the least to do with any of this.

Marshall, according to Lynn was not a violent type. "Oh yeah, Jack was a redneck and would beat you up if you started something with him a bar, but he wasn't what they made him out to be." He was just a hanger on, according to Lynn; he was just another body to help carry things and get things done and the least important member of their group. The testimony about taking out the student pilot that had been in their way was pure hogwash, he says. It had been denied by one of the government's witness but somehow still somehow figured as an example of Jack's propensity for violence. Even when he came back on appeal, Marshall, a first time offender, was once again given a stiff sentence.

None of the defendants had taken the stand. So all of the hyperbolic hooey about weapons and explosives spewed by these rascals went uncontested. The group had plenty of animosities and they openly discussed what they felt were betrayals at someone like Wood who had turned them in when they had helped him out. There had also been animosity directed at Andy's reckless pilot. But these discussions were, at worst, just grousing. Did the animosity reach the level of taking mortal sanctions against someone? No. But the government put the discussions out there, along with their assessments that these were threats to do bodily harm. It went into the stew along with all of this other talk of guns and violence.

Bagalman testified that he and Hartley flew back to Waynesboro the very next day and that when they got there they saw a crop-duster circling the load so they went back to New Orleans. But he didn't stop there. Within a few days, he said, Hartley called Bagalman and told him that they had to go to Miami because the owners needed evidence that they had not stolen the load. Armed with only a local newspaper's account, he, Fred and Lynn had flown to Miami to explain to "the Columbians" what had happened to their dope. "It was a very uncomfortable situation," Bagalman said. "We gave him the newspaper clipping. And he immediately -- he had a cellular telephone and scrambler device on it, and he called Columbia. He had some Spanish conversation and hung up and said 'Everything is going to be okay.' Then they started discussing who was going to have to pay for this particular load." The Colombians held them responsible for the lost load, he said, forcing them to fly "several" more trips for less than their normal fee. He claimed that something similar happened on another load.

Lynn could not believe his ears. "They never flew back to Waynesboro. They didn't see the crop-duster. It was in the local newspaper article. When we got there the police were already there and we just drove back to my camp and I called Fred and told him it was busted. Marks was not even present when we met Jorge to talk about the loss." It was at this point, Lynn says, that his partners extorted payment for half of the lost load and very shortly thereafter made off with another load completely. Griste told Hartley and Lynn that Valdes and his partners would pay the other half of the loss and that they would make it up on the next trip. There was no meeting with "the Columbians," not even with Lynn, who did not realize until later that the money had not been paid. "Fred and I even paid Marks half of what he would have made 'cause he was crying poor mouth and claimed he had bills he needed to take care of. Fred and I paid over $500K out of our pockets and Marks was the only crew member who even wanted money. All my guys said, 'No problem we'll make it up.'"

Justice should be about more than scalps and the body count. There is so much value placed on cooperation that the legal system has become the tail of the dog, an appendage to the practicalities of law enforcement. While it is true that the others cooperated and that Lynn's epiphany came late, there is still a serious disparity in the sentences meted out and the relative culpability of the players. Lynn was always an intermediary. It was Bill Griste, Ismael Meza, and Jorge Valdes who had the Columbian contact and that was through Fabio. Woody handled their transportation and it was through Woody that Lynn was involved. When Griste, Valdes, and Meza fell out of the picture, it was the Pruna brothers who were large and in charge. "Pablo and I didn't have much of a connection. I only dealt with him after Andy was arrested and I did three or four trips with Fernando."

Bedwell had revisited the idea of a plea with Dickie only because she was interested in allegations of public corruption, probably Jordan and the corrupt agents and Sheriff Earl Sermon Dyess, Jr. who was running Hendry County as a personal drug fiefdom. Lynn could only implicate Valdes but that would help them get Dyess, who would become the first Florida sheriff to be indicted. It would be Valdes, his partner in crime, who would bring him down. Valdes - a recidivist who claims to have been the head of the Medellin drug cartel's US operations, who profited $1 million a month and distributed 20,000 kilograms of cocaine - was released from federal prison after serving only five years. The Pruna brothers, Jordan, Griste, Ochoa, Young, Dyess, and every major player also received sweetheart deals. Every member of Lynn's gang, except Marshall, received drastically lighter sentences and everyone one of them - large fish and small - is today free, even the ones that Lynn eventually cooperated against.

Beyond that, though, there is the very salient fact that, by any usual standard in the federal legal system, Dickie Lynn has earned his second chance to, at the very least, be heard by the judge on his request for a sentence reduction. As the years have passed, there have been some changes made to the sentencing guidelines that will greatly affect Dickie's sentence. They are no longer mandatory. Thresholds have been changed. The years have also had their impact on the severity of sentences meted out by Judge Butler. And this is the real crux of the matter. Lynn may or may not deserve a sentence reduction. But that should be a matter decided by the judge who sentenced him. But, because of the manner in which the federal rules are now structured, this matter cannot be placed back before Judge Butler. Previously, either party could make a motion for a sentence reduction. Now, however, the rules limit the ability to make the initial motion for sentence reduction to only one person, the prosecutor. The gatekeeper here is Gloria Bedwell. If she does not make the motion, and she refuses to do so, then the judge is powerless to act.

The characterization of Wood as Saul on the road to Damascus is an almost universal criminal justice syndrome. It's part of the pathology that in the give-and-take of a prosecution there commonly develops a bond - not just between the defendant and his lawyer - but also between the accused and accusers, especially cooperating witnesses. Prosecutors and police officers, charged with bringing down someone that they have demonized, soon encounter a real live person and the good sometimes offsets the bad. The facts of a case, mostly unknown and initially just allegations and conjecture (and, as in this case, sometimes intentionally mischaracterized), are brought into clearer focus. More often than not, the convert turns out to be the prosecutor or the agent.

And thus it was with Ed Odom who was ultimately won over by Dickie himself. He started developing respect for Dickie on the day of his initial arrest. They took him in without incident and Odom relayed Sessions' nonnegotiable offer. Rather than be offensive, Lynn had been respectful to the officer and had even communicated a willingness to cooperate, requesting an opportunity to confer with his attorney. It seemed to Odom a reasonable request but was taken otherwise by Sessions. And Lynn's demeanor remained respectful throughout the proceedings and in all of his dealings with the agents. Each side saw that their roles were antagonistic but felt no need to be caustic.

When he traveled to Sarasota to arrest Dickie, all that he knew about Lynn was the collection of loose information that he had been amassing for three years. He relished the idea of getting the scalp of a major drug trafficker who was connected to some of the biggest names in the business. Odom had heard all manner of talk about violence and guns and murders - had seen the ghastly results of the airplane crash - and he was way-past-ready to bring these guys down. Although he cannot say for sure, he sheepishly admits that he probably wrote the original DEA report and that it contains many things that proved completely incorrect.

Odom has been in point-blank range throughout just about every facet of this case, has seen the untenable positions in which Dickie has found himself and sees him as a victim. It began early with the take-it-or-leave-it ultimatum of a blind plea to the CCE charge. Odom saw the government's scoundrels lie and cheat without being given the usual sanctions, rewarded even. He even claims that the government's concentration on the threats of violence were over-emphasized. The decision to arrest Dickie and his associates was not because of any threats of violence, he says. It was because the case had been dragging on for three years and cooperation between the United States and Colombia was starting to deteriorate to the point that they could not risk sending Abbott and Clark to Columbia. By the beginning of the trial, the agents had every reason to disbelieve just about everything that Davenport told them, including the allegations about violence. He had been caught in so many lies they would later renege on his deal.

But Dickie was still the enemy. Odom would not become Lynn's outright champion until after his arrest in Mississippi. Now charged with a new drug arrest and escape, Dickie faced trial in Hattiesburg. He and his co-defendant had strayed into a completely compromised dope deal. In his opening statement Assistant United States Attorney Peter Barrett told the jury "We're going to show you that there's no honor amongst thieves. This guy was intending to rip his partners off. He was going to steal the load and he already had it sold to another group of people," Odom recounts.

The case involved two heavy hitters from Miami, David Lemieux and Alex Decubas and their connection to Daniel Bogart, a confidential informant gone rogue. All of the conversations were being taped. Unknown to Bogart, the agents had another confidential informant inside and sensed that a double MacGuffin was brewing. Bogart was giving his handlers bogus information about the load and was actually planning to rip the shipment off. And so was Lemieux. Dickie was going to be collateral damage.

It dawned on Lynn that he had been kept from being the victim only by his arrest. He told them, "You give me 10 and let me testify to what actually went down here, I'll do it." He was sick, he said, "of being the one who got dirt shoveled on him while everyone else walked away. " Steve Bronis, now represented the other defendant. He and Roy Black made the deal. "They start immediately debriefing them. Dickie tells him the whole thing from the time he got out of Talledega. He puts it all on the table. The US Attorney in Mississippi agrees to give him 10 years and agrees to do a rule 35. They send the Rule 35 to Mobile requesting a sentence reduction and the United States Attorney's Office in Mobile refuses to do anything saying that 'He didn't do anything for us,'" Odom recaps with obvious disgust. According to Barrett, Lynn's testimony was important. "A short proffer convinced me Lynn was credible. Lynn was very valuable and I appreciate what he did. I just wish the United States Attorney's Office in the Southern District of Alabama felt the same way."

Dickie's cooperation went far beyond merely agreeing to cooperate against a man who was going to rip him off anyway. He voluntarily surrendered an additional $3 million in cash and assets, most of which were overseas and beyond the government's reach. His overall cooperation resulted in the seizure of more than $13 million in cash and assets. He continued to cooperate with the Mississippi district, even when he encountered resistance from the Southern District of Alabama. This resulted in some very valuable results, not the least of which were the extraditions of Alex Decubas from Columbia and David Lemieux from England, two targets of a major international sting called *Operation Green Ice*.

Lynn had been recaptured only because he had fallen into the search for them. Decubas, whose story makes Dickie sound like a Hardy Boy, would end up pleading to five indictments alleging that he smuggled more than 24 tons of cocaine and laundered $6.3 million in drugs profits from 1984 to 2000. Originally sentenced to thirty years, he has finished his sentence. Lemieux, the real chief, absconded to England where he would become arrested in one of that country's largest drug busts and then embroiled in a protracted extradition battle. Unlike ours, English law requires non-hearsay direct evidence in support of extradition requests. Lynn provided it and Lemieux was ultimately brought to justice in the United States. "Even for South Florida standards," a prosecutor told a Miami court, Lemieux and Decubas' activities were "absolutely exponential." Lemieux, too, is today a free man.

When more than a decade had passed and his Rule 35 request for sentence reduction still went unheeded, Barrett went over Bedwell's head. He wrote a letter to the United States Attorney for the Southern District. He urged that a Rule 35 be filed on Lynn's behalf, noting that the investigating officers in both states were in agreement and set out in detail the nature of Dickie's cooperation. The lawmakers who constantly strive to make the system intractable, who tweak the "subjectivity" out of the criminal justice system with things like the Bail Reform Act, forget that not only are defendants human but that the system is populated by individuals - judges, probation officers, prosecutors, agents, defense lawyers - who can be prey to real human foibles. Justice may be blind, but it can also be vengeful and in this regard Dickie has hit a perfect storm, a trifecta of spite that has thwarted efforts to ameliorate his sentence.

He embarrassed the United States Attorney's Office in Mobile and made "bad law" in the process. Another six years would pass after Barrett's letter. Still no action. In 2009, 20 years into his sentence, Lynn's attorney wrote Bedwell another letter. He was met with a curt response. "This office will not overlook the history of Lynn's years and years of criminal activities, including the fiery deaths of two of his smuggling pilots who crashed near Demopolis, Alabama trying to land a load of hundreds of kilograms of cocaine in the fog, threats Lynn made against law enforcement officials and others and new crimes he planned and committed after having been sentenced to life, to spare him that sentence, which he deserves."

A complaint was filed with the Department of Justice Narcotics Division, noting that "the neutral and objective perspective of the Department of Justice is required to resolve this matter justly" and requesting a brief personal meeting in Washington D.C. in order to have Barrett and the agents personally present their views. "This matter is far too important...to dismiss the issue as being in the sole discretion of Assistant United States Attorney Bedwell," the letter said. The Department of Justice referred the matter to the Mobile United States Attorney and refused to take any further action.

The Bureau of Prisons, too, had egg on its face. Lynn had escaped from their much-vaunted system. Supposedly, the head of the BOP was actually in that sally port on the day of the escape. True or not, what is important is that Dickie's escape embarrassed the agency to its very core. When two Chicago inmates escaped in 2012, the BOP bragged at how few escapes there have been from their facilities, the most recent one 11 years ago, Dickie Lynn. Odom looks for reasons to rationalize Bedwell's intransigence as being more than petulance and sanctimony. No stranger to the federal system and the fact that it can be a heartless enemy, he surmises that Dickie's past and the many allegations of his supposed involvement in violence have been part of the resistance Lynn has met in trying to mitigate his sentence.

As part of its protocol, the United States Marshals Service initiates a threat analysis whenever there has been an escape. They interviewed the agents associated with the Lynn case immediately following his flight from Talladega. They concluded that "a search of BOP information relating to Richard Lynn does not indicate the presence or suspicion of any mental illness. There is no official record of violent or bizarre behavior. Interviews conducted with investigators close to this case did not indicate the existence of any independent information relating to a threat to either the judge or the prosecutor. Dislike or even hatred of public officials does not necessarily translate into acts of violence or revenge."

On the day of his recapture in Biloxi, Dickie's beeper had gone off as he was running through the parking lot. Instinctively, he answered it. The agents, thinking he was reaching for a gun, started shooting. While the local press account and even the agents agree that he was unarmed, Dickie Lynn not only is incarcerated in a high security penitentiary, he is "on the card." As part of his Special Supervision he has been placed on the High Accountability Card and must report every two hours. This is so because, according to the BOP, Dickie "has a history of violence to include conspiring to murder a public official and firing shots at Law Enforcement during his arrest." The unsubstantiated allegations made by the government not only found their way into the PSR (pre-sentence report), they're part of his prison jacket. "He attempted," it erroneously notes, "to have a government witness killed." During the initial investigation there had been talk of a bomb being used to kill an informant. Whatever real bomb threat existed, it was not with anyone inside of the Lynn/Wood circle. It was someone connected to a conspiracy in Tampa and had been collected as ambient information in this case.

  The BOP is a large federal bureaucracy that oversees some of this country's worst criminals. It is a netherworld where the minions lurk in the shadows and do the bidding of others. What are facts and what are delusional fantasies can be hard to sort out. "A prison guard has said to him straight out, 'There are two things that you can do in the federal system that will cause you to be hated by us all, kill somebody or escape.' Everywhere that Dickie goes there is a guard that's gotten run out of Talledega because they cleaned house in Talladega," Odom says. Inmate narcissism? Probably not. And if Dickie Lynn is a bit paranoid, who can blame him? When he first arrived at Coleman USP near Tampa, he ran into a former Talladega guard who made him a promise. "I'm going to fuck you." Two days later Dickie was transferred to the Supermax in Colorado, a facility where inmates are in solitary confinement 23 hours a day. He sued the system and was eventually returned to Coleman but it didn't give Dickie any warm and fuzzies about the system.

  Prison systems are no different than the legal system. Information is the coin of the realm. A little favor here, a little gossip there, it goes a long way, especially when you're locked up forever. Whether they are self-motivated or acting at the behest of others, Lynn claims he has been targeted by other inmates who try to get him to say incriminating things like plotting vengeance against Butler or Bedwell. Even when they go nowhere, "the BOP writes reports like they're gospel," Odom says. "BOP produces a report as if it were true. That will be in his jacket forever. There is nothing he can do to get it out. Gloria was given a copy of that and as far as she's concerned he's threatened to kill her." "Let's face it. We're all, like, in this together. You're a lawyer. She's a lawyer. I'm a cop. And the bottom line is we're all supposed to be seeking the truth in these things. We ain't out to screw nobody. You ain't out to let some terror out so he can go out and terrorize. We're all here to see that justice is served. Unfortunately the whole system doesn't work like that. In Gloria's case he's tried and convicted and she don't want to hear nothing about it. To me that's wrong."

POSTSCRIPT

Show Me The Money

The law is organic. Doctrinal trunk lines define our basic notions - criminal law, property rights, marital rights, etc. -but also allow for change. Because it is based on the principal that it is Natural Law, the law can sometimes, like a moebius strip, be twisted back upon itself and used to effect wholly different, seemingly contradictory results. The United States in its infancy had been a hodgepodge in every way, a huge disconnected country of disparate parts. The railroads helped pull those parts together and did so through the vehicle of viewing property rights as expansive and monopolistic. The railroads pushed for some fairly permissive, collusive some would say, legal precedents that allowed them to gobble up necessary rights-of-ways, all under the notion of basic property rights. A century later, the NAACP legal Defense Fund and other civil rights organizations would center on those precedents, exploiting those arguments, ironically, the work of ultra capitalists, to advance equal minority rights and crystalize American civil rights law.

No more than 30 years ago a criminal prosecution only involved proving the guilt of a person. But because taking the toys away from the boys is both a lucrative resource and highly punitive sanction, the government began using what had been heretofore virtually ignored and undeveloped seizure law, eviscerating the then-common notion that private property is sacrosanct. Asset forfeiture, although it sometimes becomes the tail wagging the dog, is a ubiquitous and integral part of modern drug prosecutions. They can help gauge success and can be another source of agency friction. These groups had connections as extensive and pervasive as kudzu. The government started tracing back those links and indictments started flying out of every district that they had touched. They finally caught up with Jorge Valdes. Because of him they were able to go after the

Sheriff of Hendry County and got a slough of other druggies. They even indicted the company that sold the planes. But, mostly, they went after the money. They took Valdes' toys, his property, his father's house.

When the government arrested Lynn, they had taken his fancy cars, his really fine home on Siesta Key, his boats, motors and toters, a briefcase containing $305,000 worth of jewelry, guns, and other boy toys. This included a 1969 Corvette ZL1, one of the remaining 2 of the total of 12 ever manufactured, and valued at $260,000. The seller would testify at trial that Lynn had brought him the money in cash. It was in two attache cases, divided into hundred-thousand dollar packages, sealed in plastic and that he had spent another $200,000 in cash on other vehicles. It later netted the government more than $300,000 at auction. The search of a Lynn family member's home had revealed a Swiss bank account with several million dollars in it. They went after everything. A real estate broker in Panama City, Florida, had known Deshaw for several years. Charged with money laundering and now cooperating, he testified that Lynn had given him $650,000 in cash in a suitcase and that Deshaw had also given him $200,000 to "invest," in return for a six percent fee. All of the defendants relinquished large sums of money. But the agents knew that some of it was hidden and they followed the trails.

"There was a lot of money out there and I stayed on the real conservative side of it. Dickie cleared somewhere around $1 million a load after he paid everyone." In his debriefing William Wood had told the agents about his Cayman Island banking connections. Those bribe payments Carol Wood made were connected to Inco bank in the Caymans. Their mortgage was to Inco bank. Other financial records, most importantly Dickie Lynn's, showed a connection to that bank. Chris Bain, the president of the bank would be indicted in the Northern District of Florida. In the end, the group would enmesh the entire international banking system in a financial scandal involving drug proceeds. It would begin in 1990 when a South Florida federal grand jury issued a money laundering indictment against Fernando Pruna claiming that he and others had funneled $200 million in drug profits through a string of overseas bank accounts and phony corporations. The grand jury started subpoenaing bank records and the ramifications were worldwide. In 2000 the Irish government, concerned about the implications for what are there considered venerable institutions, constituted the Moriarty Tribunal which held hearings investigating these and other allegations about money-laundering in Europe.

The Guinness and Mahan Bank in Dublin and its subsidiaries in the Caymans were accused of being accomplices to Fernando and Andy Pruna's activities. How was it, the Irish committee wanted to know, that the Prunas and some of their associates had gotten million-dollar loans underwritten by a European bank? And it went beyond mere willful blindness; there were allegations of false documents having been made with the active involvement of the bank. The Irish judicial system issued the extensive Ansbacher Report fully documenting what it found to be criminal and dubious practices that had led to the banking abuses, a section which concerned "The Pruna Affair."

Fabio Ochoa

Wood had initially baited the hook with two names, Pablo Escobar and Fabio Ochoa. The agents were understandably excited. Ultimately the trail would lead to Jorge Valdes and Ismael Meza and, through them, Pablo Escobar. The cartel leader, the focus of an international police hunt, would be gunned down by the Columbian authorities. Fabio? Well, it turns out that there are two Fabio Ochoas and the Columbian that was Wood's connection wasn't much. Or, at least, not yet.

Fabio Enrique Ochoa Vasquez, the one connected to the Barry Seal assassination, was not Fabio Enrique Ochoa Vasco. Wood's connection was a relatively minor player. (So as to avoid confusion he later changed his name to Carlos Mario.) Born in 1960 in Columbia, his family moved to Miami. By the time he was 18, he was dealing in major quantities of drugs.

By the age 29 he had already done time in Oklahoma and was the focus of several federal indictments: a 1981 marijuana indictment in Miami that named him, his brother Mauricio, William Griste, Wood, and others. With the Alabama case and indictments in two Florida districts looming over him, this little cork of a man fled Miami, a city he had known since the age of two and went back to his mother country. It was a wise career move. He became intimately connected with major Medellin Cartel figures such as Luis Fernando Galeano Berrio, Gerardo "Kike" Moncada, Diego Fernando Murillo Bejarano (a.k.a. "Don Berna"), and, yes, even the notorious Pablo Escobar Gaviria himself.

By 2004, though, he had become enough of a problem for US authorities in his own right. He was indicted for narcotics trafficking and money laundering, this time in the Middle District of Florida. Like the other Columbian drug kingpins, he had become intimately involved in his country's politics and its brutal internal war. He was by now one of the "extraditables" over which the United States and Columbia tussled. On March 28, 2007 the United States placed a $5 million reward on his head, naming him a principal individual on the United States Department of the Treasury's Office of Foreign Assets Control (OFAC) list of Specially Designated Narcotics Traffickers (SDNTs), targeting also 45 companies and 64 individuals across Colombia, Belize, Ecuador, Guatemala, Honduras, Jamaica, Mexico, and Panama that the government maintained were really part of his network.

By 2009, Ochoa had orchestrated his surrender and on September 9, 2009, now 48 years old, entered into a plea agreement to a charge that carried a 20 year maximum. That is no small concession considering that federal conspiracy counts, even for first time offenders, carry a mandatory minimum of 10 years and a maximum of life. Ochoa, a top-level manager and recidivist, who acknowledged importing from 6 to 8 tons of cocaine MONTHLY, avoided the risk of a recalcitrant judge hammering him. He also agreed to forfeit $15 million in cash and property. (Do the math.)

How Ochoa managed his deal is open to conjecture. However, Columbian news accounts indicate that he ratted out the *Autodefensas Unidades de Colombia* (AUC), the paramilitary organization that has been identified by the US as a Foreign Terrorist Organization. Perhaps it's a coincidence that *Don Berna*, Ochoa's benefactor, was also extradited in 2009. Accused of being an AUC leader guilty of aggravated homicides and the "forced disappearance" of 67 people (including children as young as 13 years old), "forced displacement" and multiple conspiracies, he pleaded guilty to drug trafficking charges and was sentenced in New York in 2009, where he currently remains imprisoned. On June 5, 2010 Ochoa was sentenced to 17½ years and fined $15 million. He is listed as "not in BOP custody."

Roy Black

During the trial, Bedwell had accused both Bronis and Black of conflicts of interest due to their representation of other defendants, some of them connected to the case. Black had defended Salvador Magluta who was tied to Dyess and Valdes. Lynn would later hire Bronis to represent him on appeal, causing the government to file another conflict of interest motion. Subsequent investigations relating to the money laundering aspects of the prosecution and drug proceeds, the government said, showed that Lynn had directed the transfer of money from Switzerland to pay for Bronis' fee for Eyster's representation. Black would also represent Lynn in the Mississippi prosecution and it would be Bronis who would represent Lynn's co-defendant there.

Ultimately, Black would end up representing Ochoa and this would end up getting him ensnared. Black's fee for representing Ochoa was $5 million, a third of the amount Ochoa would eventually agree to forfeit in his plea bargain. In Miami the government routinely requests what's called a *Nibbia* hearing, an investigation into the source of a lawyer's fees. One can have the fee forfeited or, worse yet, be caught up in a money-laundering or drug prosecution. Black, knowing what all criminal defense lawyers know, that his would be a wonderful scalp for any law enforcement officer or prosecutor's belt, hired Ben Kuehne to vet his fee, agreeing to pay him a $175,000 fee.

Kuehne, a past President of the Miami-Dade County Bar Association, a member of the Board of Governors of the Florida Bar and one of Al Gore's attorneys during the Florida recount, is an esteemed member of the bar. He traveled to Columbia and assured himself that the money was from legitimate sources and reported back favorably to Black. Kuehne became one of those scalps. His indictment for conspiracy to launder money set off a national wave of protests within the criminal defense bars that accused the government of overreaching and was only resolved by a favorable Eleventh Circuit appeal.

Gloria Bedwell

In early 1992, the Justice Department honored Bedwell with the Exceptional Service Award. In presenting her the Department of Justice's highest award for employee performance, Attorney General William Barr noted that over a three-year period, she had served as the single case attorney prosecuting three major international drug smuggling cases, one of those the Lynn case. "As a result of her dedication and skills," the citation read, "these smuggling organizations were destroyed, 94 defendants were convicted with five receiving life sentences and over $6 million forfeited." *The Tuscaloosa News*, Bedwell's hometown paper, reported the remarks of Jeff Sessions, who lauded "her mastery of the complexities of the law relating to international smuggling cases and forfeitures, her willingness to work long hours and her determination not to stop until every member of the organization has been sentenced to long terms in jail and all their assets are stripped." Today, she still plugs along, putting bad guys in jail.

CHRONOLOGY

11/1/1979	William Wood's first involvement with smuggling, offloaded of marijuana from freighter off southern coast of Florida.
5/4/1982	Wood Arrested in Florida on state charge of Trafficking in Marijuana.
9/1/1982	Wood and Ricou Deshaw do marijuana airdrops from Jamaica into waters off the coast of Florida.
10/1/1982	Wood gets involved in smuggling cocaine.
3/5/1983	Wood incarcerated in Charlotte County (Florida) jail for 4 months.
6/1/1984	While both working as off loaders, Wood and Dickie Lynn run into each other.
10/14/1984	Amber II, a Louisiana corporation incorporated by attorney Marks Bagalman takes delivery of aircraft N-15WW in New Orleans.
5/1/1985	MEETING: Bagalman meets with others to discuss marijuana smuggling.
7/15/1985	DOPE DEAL: Bagalman, Fred Hartley, Deshaw and Lynn set out from New Orleans airport. Go in two airplanes to Belize.
7/16/1985	Dickie and Ricou crash plane in Belize. Other plane arrives safely.
7/18/1985	Deshaw and Lynn arrive in New Orleans on a commercial flight. Customs Inspector Jerome Long questions them. When a false-bottomed compartment is found in an attache case, they are detained for a short while. Copies all of their information, including address book and aircraft documents, are made and given to Customs Agent Wicks. Agent Wicks tries to follow them but they give him the slip.
7/18/1985	BOLO: Customs has the FAA "be on the lookout for" aircraft N840BK.

7/19/1985	Wicks cancels BOLO, informs FAA that N840BK had been destroyed.
8/1/1985	INDICTMENT: Fabio Enrique Ochoa, Wood, and William Griste and William Wood indicted for cocaine importations from Columbia through Bahamas into South Florida. Southern District of Florida, Miami.
8/28/1985	INDICTMENT: Charles Jordan and 27 others, indicted for marijuana importations into Louisiana. Eastern District of Louisiana, 85cr321.
9/11/1985	DOPE DEAL: One of the eight Ochoa, Griste, and Wood importations.
9/21/1985	Hartley, Bagalman, Deshaw, Lynn fly to Chicago to buy aircraft N-711KZ.
10/1/1985	Lynn and Deshaw also buy an airplane (N-15WW) to replace BK, using Bagalman as a straw man and naming Amber II corporation as the owner.
10/1/1985	Wood's group flies 500 kilograms of cocaine from Colombia to Marsh Harbour, Bahamas.
10/22/1985	Bagalman enters rehab.
11/9/1985	Schmidgall and Eyster monitor communications for Wood Bahamas/Key Largo run of 325 kilos of coke.
11/30/1985	Bagalman discharged from rehab in Pensacola.
12/1/1985	(Approximate date) Wood and his brother-in-law Howard Carrell fly to Alabama to check out landing strip. Lynn and Deshaw are there.
12/1/1985	SURVEILLANCE: (Approximate date) Agents' stakeout on N711KZ shows Bagalman and Hartley flying the plane.
12/15/1985	DOPE DEAL: Wood and Hartley fly N-15WW out of Tamiami to Monteria, Columbia and then to Orange Walk where they are

Apprehended: The Trials of Dickie Lynn

met by Ricou.

12/16/1985   Wood and Hartley fly 521 Keys into Sumpter County, Alabama for Woody and Ochoa.

1/1/1986   DOPE DEAL: Aborted Ochoa and Wood dope deal from Jamaica, chased by Air Force jets.

3/1/1986   DOPE DEAL: Bagalman and Hartley fly another dope trip.

4/22/1986   INDICTMENT: Fred Pou, et al., Eastern District of Louisiana, New Orleans, 86cr00182.

6/1/1986   ARREST: Michael Stanton is questioned by Missouri police regarding allegations that he is involved in the distribution of cocaine. Fearing a search of his home, he puts the contraband in a backpack and asks his son and a friend to hide the backpack for him in the woods. Stanton later retrieved the backpack and delivered it to Wood, who claimed that some of the cocaine was missing. Stanton was arrested for threatening the kids. He was subsequently charged with State and federal drug offenses.

6/5/1986   REJECTED: Senate votes against Jeff Sessions' nomination as federal judge. (Nominated 10/85)

6/11/1986   INDICTMENT: Inco, a Cayman Islands Bank, and Chris Bain, one of its officers, are indicted for Money Laundering in the Northern District of Florida.

6/22/1986   DOPE DEAL: Authorities in Waynesboro, Mississippi find sixteen burlap sacks containing 711 kilo bricks of cocaine left abandoned by the side of an airstrip. Two more large sacks containing smaller bricks of cocaine had been dragged into the woods off the side of the runway. An investigation ensues to determine what had happened but no arrests follow.

7/1/1986   INTERVIEW/DEBRIEFING: Stanton begins cooperating with the government and discloses Wood's role in the conspiracy.

7/1/1986   Fred Hartley has an accident in Belize and dings up the aircraft.

Apprehended: The Trials of Dickie Lynn

7/1/1986	INDICTMENT: Celestino Mendez, et al., District of Maine, Bangor, 86cr52.
7/29/1986	ARREST: Wood is arrested by Customs at the St. Petersburg-Clearwater Airport and charged with conspiracy to falsely register an aircraft. Using a false name, he had been trying to pick up a jet airplane that he had paid for with $1,085,000 in cash.
7/31/1986	INDICTMENT: Wood is indicted in St Louis for a cocaine conspiracy.
9/1/1986	Tom McVay's name comes up. Leads agents to N117EV.
10/20/1986	TRIAL: Wood trial begins in St Louis.
11/21/1986	SENTENCE: Wood sentenced to 20 years in Missouri.
12/1/1986	DOPE DEAL: Bagalman's plane used in deal.
1/6/1987	Bagalman enters rehab at Kennedy Institute.
1/7/1987	Frank Basso pays bribe to help Wood.
2/20/1987	Carol Wood makes first of seven bribes that would total $1.4 million.
5/22/1987	Basso tries to make another delivery of bribe money but is put off by agents.
6/4/1987	Carol Wood pays $50,000 in Orlando.
6/19/1987	Fred Pou is moving his operation to an airstrip that he is building on the Belize/Mexico/Honduras border. Worried about the possibility of bandits, he approaches Bob Wardle about providing security for that airstrip.
6/21/1987	DOPE DEAL: Clark and Abbott fly from Tamiami in N15WW to Columbia and return with 600 keys.
6/22/1987	They land in Demopolis (Lynn, Marshall, Andy, Purvis,

Apprehended: The Trials of Dickie Lynn

McKeown, Eyster, Deweese).

7/19/1987	Davenport travels by commercial air to Belize to help Wardle set up security for a new load.
7/21/1987	The trip is scrubbed. Wardle and Davenport return to the States.
7/30/1987	Basso meets with undercover agent in Boca Raton, Florida.
7/31/1987	Basso is recorded making a bribe on Wood's behalf.
8/19/1987	Basso is recorded in another undercover conversation.
8/21/1987	Wood writes a letter from the Ashland, Kentucky penitentiary implicating himself in the bribery attempt.
8/28/1987	Basso, again, is caught on tape in Miami trying to bribe the undercover agents on Wood's behalf.
9/1/1987	Abbott travels to Belize to look at a new airstrip. ("The Queen" had been bombed.)
9/1/1987	SURVEILLANCE: Labor Day stakeout of N117EV in New Orleans.
9/3/1987	Abbott departs Belize.
9/23/1987	Carol Wood delivers $210,000 bribe money in Orlando. (The following day she closes out one of her safe deposit boxes. It had only been open 2 days.)
9/24/1987	Abbott travels to Miami where he and Clark plan to make seven trips in tandem with Hartley.
9/25/1987	DOPE DEAL: N117EV crash-lands at Demopolis Airport in Alabama, exploding into a ball of fire. Dental records later identified the burned body of the pilot, found by the roadside, as Fred Hartley. The body of the pilot's brother, Joe Hartley, was found charred inside the wreckage. Two hundred thirteen red and green packages containing cocaine were found all over the road. Again, an investigation did not produce any immediate arrests.

9/27/1987	INTERVIEW: Bagalman is interviewed by Wicks (does not cooperate).
9/29/1987	INDICTMENT: Charles Jordan and others are charged with marijuana offenses in the Eastern District of Louisiana.
10/2/1987	Carol Wood delivers $86,300 of the bribe money to undercover agent.
10/10/1987	DOPE DEAL: Another load crashes in Belize.
10/11/1987	INDICTMENT: Jordan, Wallace and other Customs agents are indicted in the Southern District of Florida, Miami.
10/13/1987	Agent Miller has an undercover conversation with Basso regarding bribery arrangements.
10/16/1987	Warrants issue from Tampa for Wood, Carol Wood, Basso, Koons and David Carlson for attempted bribery of government officials involving $1.4 million.
10/16/1987	INDICTMENT: Charles Jordan, et al, charged in the Southern District of Florida.
10/23/1987	ARREST: Carol Wood is arrested in the Florida Keys and remains detained for 6 or 7 weeks.
11/11/1987	INTERVIEW/DEBRIEF: David Carlson, one of William Wood's pilots, tells Customs Agent Donald Schmidt that he flew a person he knew as "Chris" from Florida to Alabama. Carlson further identified him as a former commercial airline pilot and a counter-surveillance specialist who utilized a spectrum analyzer for monitoring law enforcement frequencies.
11/19/1987	INTERVIEW/DEBRIEFING: William Wood gives initial interview at Ashland federal penitentiary in Kentucky and details the Alabama operation.
12/29/1987	INTERVIEW/DEBRIEF: Howard Carrell, Wood's brother-in-law, identifies Schmidgall as the radio operator for the marijuana airdrops in Florida and gives details of the Alabama

importation, but does not identify Schmidgall as a participant in that venture.

1/1/1988   MEETING: Bagalman meets with the United States Attorney in New Orleans who proposes deal if he'll plead. He turns it down.

1/2/1988   BOLO: Customs (Long) has FAA "be on the look out for" aircraft N3550K and N117EV.

1/12/1988 DEBRIEF: Wood is debriefed again. He provides yet more details about the Alabama venture. He relates how he and his copilot were in constant radio contact with Schmidgall, who was at the hunting camp in Sumter County and implicates Steve Purvis.

1/21/1988 INTERVIEW: Customs agents visit Schmidgall's house. He refuses to cooperate. They take notice of the communications towers at the home.

1/26/1988 INTERVIEW/DEBRIEF: Schmidgall is interviewed in Miami by law enforcement agents from the Southern District of Florida.

1/28/1988 A search warrant for Dennis Martin Aviation in Ft. Lauderdale is issued. (CI-4 in the affidavit is Wood.)

1/31/1988 Davenport travels by commercial air to Belize. He brings money and equipment.

2/27/1988 Davenport travels by commercial air to Belize again.

3/23/1988 TRIAL: The trial of eight defendants begins in Miami without Charles Jordan who has absconded.

3/27/1988 Davenport travels by commercial air to Belize.

4/7/1988   Abbott returns from Belize.

4/22/1988 INTERVIEW/DEBRIEFING: Wood is debriefed in great detail by the government agents. This 60-hour session lasted until April 29 and yielded a 31-page report.

4/22/1988	INDICTMENT: Celestino Mendez, District of Maine, 88cr12.
5/3/1988	N711KZ is seized by Customs.
5/9/1988	Wardle travels to Mexico.
5/18/1988	Davenport travels by commercial air to Belize.
5/27/1988	Davenport travels to Mexico.
6/1/1988	INDICTMENT: John R. Harrison, *et al*, indicted for cocaine conspiracy. Harrison's source is Wood through Michael Stanton. Wood and Stanton end up testifying against Harrison.
6/2/1988	Davenport travels by commercial air to Belize. The trip is scrubbed.
6/10/1988	INDICTMENT: Celestino Mendez, District of Maine 88cr22.
6/12/1988	Wardle and Davenport meet with CI at Tuskeegee to see about getting his help in recovering load in Belize.
6/21/1988	Wardle picks up money from Deweese and travels to Mexico and then Belize.
6/22/1988	DOPE DEAL: A load from Columbia lands on a cane field road. Clark and Abbott, the pilots, give Wardle $43,000 and a weapon for Pou. They land their load in Alabama. (McKeown, Abbott, Clark, Wardle, Davenport, Purvis, Sheehy, Deweese)
6/29/1988	Wardle leaves, departing from Mexico.
8/18/1988	SENTENCE: Marden, one of Jordan's co-defendants, is sentenced to seven years in the Southern District of Florida case.
8/19/1988	INDICTMENT: Fernando Pruna, Andres Pruna, Charles Jordan, et al., Southern District of Florida, 88cr00551.
10/1/1988	Tony Chambless signs a plea agreement in the Northern District of Alabama, agrees to work undercover.

Apprehended: The Trials of Dickie Lynn

10/20/1988	DEBRIEFING: Agents and prosecutors interview Chambless, an Alabamian who was involved in the December 1985 importation.
11/6/1988	UNDERCOVER RECORDING: Chambless and Dick Turpin.
11/9/1988	UNDERCOVER RECORDING: Chambless and Turpin.
11/20/1988	UNDERCOVER RECORDING: Chambless and Deshaw.
11/22/1988	Wardle flies to Sarasota to get rest of money Pou is owed from Lynn, continues to Cancun.
12/5/1988	DEBRIEFING: Agents and prosecutors interview Schmidgall, who agrees to continue the session the next day but he never returns.
12/8/1988	UNDERCOVER RECORDING: Chambless and Deshaw.
12/10/1988	DOPE DEAL: Marion, Alabama police respond to a call about unusual activity at a small airstrip called Vaiden Field in Perry County. They arrive at the airstrip, their blue lights flashing, just as a plane is departing. The plane heads directly toward them, forcing them to swerve to avoid a collision. The plane escapes into the night. They focus on the load vehicle and the persons on the ground. They give chase but seize only a pick-up truck and its contents.
12/11/1988	Agents trace a Cessna 404 Titan (N165SA) to Muscle Shoals Airport in the northern part of the state and question the pilots as they prepare to board a commercial flight. Two weeks later, Patrick Abbott and Robert Clark would obtain immunity from prosecution in exchange for information on their activities and their cooperation in obtaining further evidence.
12/12/1988	UNDERCOVER RECORDING: Chambless and Deshaw (Ex 29).
1/1/1989	PLEA: Barclay, a minor player in the Alabama schemes, pleads guilty.
1/30/1989	UNDERCOVER RECORDING: Chambless and Deshaw and

Deshaw's father.

2/1/1989	INDICTMENT: Ochoa, Deshaw, Schmidgall, Northern District of Alabama, 2:1989-cr-00018, Birmingham.
2/13/1989	INTERVIEW: Dick Turpin is questioned by a private investigator hired by Lynn's attorney.
2/14/1989	INTERVIEW: Chambless is questioned by Lynn's private investigator.
2/17/1989	DEBRIEFING: Wood puts it on Schmidgall. (See his affidavit.)
2/20/1989	UNDERCOVER RECORDING: Clark makes clandestine tape of Lynn.
2/21/1989	UNDERCOVER RECORDING: Clark makes clandestine tape of Lynn.
2/23/1989	INDICTMENT (Sealed): Lynn, Deshaw, Eyster, Marshall, Keaser, et al., Southern District of Alabama, 89cr00072, Mobile.
3/2/1989	UNDERCOVER RECORDING: Clark makes clandestine tape of Lynn.
3/3/1989	Wardle & Davenport meet Lynn in Atlanta Ramada to discuss another trip and to look at strips in Alabama. Wardle is shown papers concerning Alabama investigation.
3/5/1989	Clark makes clandestine tape of Lynn.
3/6/1989	Wardle goes on to Cancun.
3/8/1989	Odom and Co stake out Lynn's wife's car which was parked at Tampa airport.
3/9/1989	Lynn arrives at the airport to pick up Purvis and they pick up his tail.
3/14/1989	UNDERCOVER RECORDING: Clark makes a clandestine tape of Lynn.

Apprehended: The Trials of Dickie Lynn

3/15/1989	UNDERCOVER RECORDING: Clark makes clandestine tape of Lynn, Purvis, & Abbott.
4/24/1989	*Project 8916*, part of something called *Stargate,* is tasked with finding Charles Jordan using the paranormal technique of "remote viewing."
4/26/1989	UNDERCOVER RECORDING: Clark makes a clandestine tape of Lynn.
4/27/1989	Agents follow Deweese and Lynn from Ocean Blvd home. (See Odom Affidavit.)
5/1/1989	UNDERCOVER RECORDING: Clark makes a clandestine tape of Lynn.
5/5/1989	Davenport meets with Lynn to get $10,000 for refueling. Talk of "eliminating" someone.
5/6/1989	Lynn is Arrested. Davenport is arrested.
5/9/1989	INDICTMENT UNSEALED: Lynn, Deshaw, Eyster, Marshall, Keaser, et al., Southern District of Alabama, 89cr00072, Mobile.
5/10/1989	Detention Hearing is held in Miami for Deshaw, Eyster, Deweese, and Butch McKeown.
5/16/1989	Wood testifies for government in Oklahoma case.
5/16/1989	INDICTMENT: Ochoa, Mauricio Ochoa, Sawyer, Griste, Schmidgall, Eyster, *et al.*, Southern District of Florida, 89cr00284, Miami.
5/30/1989	Carrell testifies before a Tampa Grand Jury.
6/16/1989	ARRESTED: Charles Jordan is arrested in Pinedale, Wyoming by John William Juhasz.
8/23/1989	DEBRIEFING: Agent Coram interviews Steve Purvis. Purvis confirms previously revealed aspects of Schmidgall's

participation.

8/25/1989	INDICTMENT: Christian Schmidgall, et al., Middle District of Florida, 89cr00179, Tampa.
9/7/1989	PLEA: Deweese.
9/7/1989	PLEA: Wardle.
9/8/1989	SENTENCE: Celestino Mendez sentenced in Bangor, Maine.
9/8/1989	PLEA: Davenport.
9/12/1989	TRIAL: Lynn, Deshaw, Eyster, Marshall, and Keaser go to trial, Southern District of Alabama, 89cr00072, Mobile.
10/2/1989	DEBRIEF: Sheehy interviewed in Tampa by Dunn and Schmidt.
10/2/1989	Bagalman signs plea agreement to testify against Lynn and Deshaw
10/11/1989	INDICTMENT: Superceding indictment adds Andy Pruna. (Jordan recently arrested - had been a fugitive for 3 years.) Southern District of Florida, Miami.
10/17/1989	VERDICT: Jury convicts Lynn, Eyster, and Marshall but acquits Deshaw and Keaser. Southern District of Alabama, Mobile, 89cr00072.
11/3/1989	SENTENCE: Wardle is sentenced to 120 months.
12/15/1989	SENTENCE: Lynn is sentenced to life imprisonment without parole.
12/15/1989	SENTENCE: Eyster sentenced to 204 months.
12/15/1989	SENTENCE: Marshall sentenced to 293 months.
12/29/1989	Lynn arrives at Talladega FCI.
1/5/1990	SENTENCE: Barclay is sentenced to 48 months.

Apprehended: The Trials of Dickie Lynn

1/5/1990	SENTENCE: Deweese is sentenced to 168 months.
1/5/1990	SENTENCE: Davenport is sentenced to 120 months.
3/23/1990	Lynn and Fowler escape from Talladega Federal Prison.
4/13/1990	The abandoned truck that had been used in the prison breakout is found in Adairsville, Georgia.
4/27/1990	Fowler is captured at a bar in Atlanta.
6/1/1990	INDICTMENT: Fabio Enrique Ochoa, et al., Middle District of Florida, 89cr00179, Tampa.
7/19/1990	INDICTMENT: Bagalman, Lynn, Deshaw, Pou and Lloyd Randall, Eastern District of Louisiana, 90cr00295, New Orleans.
7/30/1990	INDICTMENT: Fernando Pruna, Southern District of Florida, 90cr00490, Miami.
8/17/1990	Lynn's Appeal dismissed.
8/29/1990	Lynn Recaptured.
8/30/1990	INDICTMENT: Jorge Valdes and Ismael Meza indicted in the Southern District of Alabama for conspiracy to import and distribute cocaine.
11/14/1990	INDICTMENT: Deshaw, Southern District of Florida, 90cr00890, Miami.
12/5/1990	INDICTMENT: Schmidgall, Northern District of Alabama, 90cr00261, Birmingham.
12/5/1990	INDICTMENT: Deshaw, Northern District of Alabama 90cr00262, Birmingham.
1/15/1991	INDICTMENT: Andy Pruna, Southern District of Florida, 91cr00018, Miami.
1/30/1991	SENTENCE REDUCTION MOTION: Miami US Attorney files

a Rule 35 for Sheehy based on his cooperation against Ricou.

3/6/1991	INDICTMENT: Bagalman, et al., Northern District of Alabama, 91cr00052, Birmingham.
3/26/1991	SENTENCE: Andy Pruna is sentenced to 12 years concurrent with other cases, Southern District of Florida, 91cr00018, Miami.
4/17/1991	RELEASED: William Griste is released from federal custody.
5/7/1991	The government of the Bahamas sends a letter detailing Sheehy's cooperation regarding the 1985 loads and its investigation into government corruption there.
6/10/1991	SENTENCE REDUCTION MOTION: Bedwell files an addendum to the Rule 35 for Sheehy based on the request of the Bahamas.
12/4/91	SENTENCE: Jorge Valdes sentenced to ten years concurrent with other sentence.
12/17/1991	Eyster and Marshall's convictions are overturned.
1/31/1992	Gloria Bedwell receives the DOJ's Exceptional Service Award.
5/28/1992	INDICTMENT: Deshaw, Northern District of Alabama, 92cr00136, Birmingham.
7/27/1992	PLEA: Eyster pleads.
7/31/1992	PLEA: Marshall pleads.
8/7/1992	SENTENCE: Marshall is re-sentenced to 235 months.
9/29/1992	SENTENCE: Eyster is re-sentenced to 120 months.
10/23/1992	INDICTMENT: Fernando Pruna, Southern District of Florida, 92cr00656, Miami.
2/3/1993	PLEA: Hendry County Sheriff Earl Sermon Dyess, Jr. pleads guilty in Ft. Meyers to being involved in a cocaine conspiracy

with Jorge Valdes and Ismael Meza. He would be released from Federal custody after five years.

2/19/1993   SENTENCE REDUCTION: Wardle's sentence reduced to 96 months.

4/9/1993   RELEASED: Howard Carrell released from Federal custody.

4/15/1993   SENTENCED: Hendry County Sheriff Earl Sermon Dyess, Jr. sentenced to 17 ½ years for his part in the Valdes, Meza cocaine conspiracy.

4/19/1993   SENTENCE: Fernando Pruna sentenced to 12 years to run concurrently with sentence in other cases, Southern District of Florida, 92cr00656, Miami.

7/14/1994   PLEA: Southern District of Florida, 94cr00340, Ricou Deshaw.

9/8/1994   RELEASED: Marks Bagalman released from Federal custody.

9/22/1994   RELEASED: Wood released from Federal custody.

12/28/1994   SENTENCE REDUCTION: Pruna sentence reduced to 10 years.

12/29/1994   RELEASED: Andy Pruna released from Federal custody.

1/18/1995   SENTENCE: Southern District of Florida, 94cr00340 Ricou Deshaw 5 years, sentence to run concurrent with sentence imposed in case 94cr341 and 90cr890 and with sentence now serving in case 90cr295.

1/18/1995   SENTENCE: Southern District of Florida, 94cr00341 Ricou Deshaw 14 years, sentence to run concurrent with sentence imposed in case 94cr340 and 90cr890 and with sentence now serving in case 90cr295.

3/5/1995   RELEASED: Jorge Valdes released from federal prison custody, paroled after serving five years.

4/25/1995   INDICTMENT: Marks Bagalman, Eastern District of Louisiana, 95cr00141, New Orleans.

Apprehended: The Trials of Dickie Lynn

5/26/1995	RELEASED: Charles Frank Jordan released from Federal custody.
8/7/1995	RELEASED: Robert Irving Eyster released from Federal custody.
6/12/1996	RELEASED: Earl Sermon Dyess Jr. released from Federal custody.
6/25/1996	RELEASED: Kevin Sheehy released from Federal custody.
9/16/1996	SENTENCE REDUCTION MOTION: Fernando Pruna (followed by 6 sealed motions, last one 12/20/96).
9/17/1996	RELEASED: Fernando Pruna released from Federal custody.
4/28/1998	Bagalman dies.
5/8/1998	RELEASED: Christian Schmidgall released from Federal custody
6/12/1996	RELEASED: Hendry County Sheriff Earl Sermon Dyess, Jr. released from Federal custody.
6/11/2001	DISMISSED: Fabio Ochoa, government files motion to dismiss, Northern District of Alabama, 89cr00018, Birmingham.
10/29/2001	DISMISSED: Fabio Ochoa, government files motion to dismiss, Middle District of Florida 89cr00179, Tampa.
7/8/2002	RELEASED: Deshaw released from Federal custody.
8/12/2003	RELEASED: Daniel Bogart released from Federal custody.
3/28/2007	NAMED: Fabio Enrique Ochoa Vasco (a.k.a."Carlos Mario"), named principal individual on list of Specially Designated Narcotics Traffickers (SDNT).
9/18/2007	RELEASED: Marshall released from Federal Custody.
7/31/2009	PLEA: Fabio Ochoa pleads guilty to an importation that is

capped at a 20-year maximum, Middle District of Florida, 09cr83.

9/9/2009   PLEA: Fabio Ochoa, plus $15 million, Middle District of Florida, 04cr374, Tampa.

6/5/2010   SENTENCE: Fabio Ochoa, 17.5 years, Middle District of Florida, 04cr374, Tampa.

8/9/2011   RELEASED: David Lemieux released from Federal custody.

6/14/2012 RELEASED: Alex Decubas released from Federal custody.